"I Can Never Forget"

PRESENTED TO
THE GLENVIEW PUBLIC LIBRARY
in honor of

the Golden Anniversary of the

- 442 nd -
Regimental Combat Team

From: Ann Yoshida

For the gallant
nisei soldiers
of World War II
especially for those
whose voices
are missing

"I Can Never Forget"

MEN OF THE 100TH/442ND

Thelma Chang

SIGI PRODUCTIONS, INC.

SIGI PRODUCTIONS, INC.
P.O. Box 26390
Honolulu, HI 96825

Designed by Steve Shrader
Typeset by Typehouse Hawaii
Edited by Cheryl Chee Tsutsumi
Printed by Toppan Printing
    Company, Singapore

Library of Congress Catalog
Card Number: 91-90350
ISBN Number: 0-9630228-0-6

Second Printing, 1991

Printed in Singapore

Contents

Corporal Daniel K. Inouye, E Company, 2nd Battalion. Inouye earned a Distinguished Service Cross for valor. The 2nd Battalion was awarded two Presidential Unit Citations.

Introduction

ISTORIES OF WAR or significant battles are usually written by presidents and prime ministers, by great generals and admirals, or by diplomats and intelligence specialists. This extraordinary book, "I Can Never Forget": Men of the 100th/442nd, written by Thelma Chang, covers a small part, albeit an important part, of World War II as seen and recalled by combat soldiers. It is moving and poignant; but like all wars as seen through the eyes of soldiers, it is at times earthy, coarse and bloody. For those interested in the unique experiences and contributions of Japanese American soldiers in World War II, this is a "must-read" book.

Daniel K. Inouye
United States Senator

(Upper left) D Company, 100th Battalion. (R) Barney Miyazono. Soldier at left is unidentified.
(Upper right) Akira Fukuda and Lizo Honma, Antitank Company. Italy, Spring 1945. (Lower left)
Sakato Okamoto and "Dutchie" Sekomoto, K Company, 3rd Battalion. Maritime Alps, January 1945.
(Lower right) Henry "Clappy" Yamane, Antitank Company, and a medic friend, 100th Battalion.

Foreword

THE STORIES OF JAPANESE AMERICANS in World War II have been told and retold, but there seems to be an endless reserve of wonderful and terrible accounts. I can still remember my exhilaration, as a teenager in the 1950s, of seeing *Go For Broke* at the Waikiki Theater. Even with Van Johnson as the lead, these were "my people" portrayed as heroes and fools, idealists and cynics, the fiery and docile, the eloquent and inarticulate. Then, we were too young to understand that one of the reasons we discussed the film well into the night over ice cream sodas at a local drive-in was the movie's extraordinary departure from our staple fare of John Wayne-type treatments of the evil "Jap" stereotypes on the screen.

Thelma Chang has brought to life many individual accounts of the young men who went to war—many of them from Hawaii where their families continued to live under unequal conditions, and others from the Mainland where they volunteered from American-style concentration camps.

There are stories reminiscent of those told in other books about the *nisei* soldiers, but this book reminds me more of the award-winning films by Loni Ding—*Nisei Soldier* and *Color of Honor*. Perhaps it is no accident that second-generation Japanese American veterans (the *nisei*) could more freely express their feelings to Asian American women of another generation. And perhaps it took nearly half a century before some of these feelings could be made public. Many of the men have never recounted memories of training and combat except to others who shared their experiences. Their families will be grateful because the war was critical in the shaping of that entire generation, and this work brings them closer to us.

It was actually therapeutic, for example, to feel the anger in Tadao Beppu's account of having to wear a special badge with black borders that identified Americans of Japanese ancestry who worked in "sensitive" jobs. And it was interesting to note the confusion of Germans who wondered why these men with Asian faces were fighting for "the Americans."

This is a carefully crafted book. Sources were scrupulously checked and rechecked; the feelings of the interviewees and their families were honored. Nonetheless, readers will find new information and insights that are revealing of the people and the time.

Franklin Odo, Ph.D
Director of Ethnic Studies
University of Hawaii at Manoa

Lieutenant Walter T. Matsumoto, 232nd Combat Engineer Company. Spring 1944.

To Mother:
Love
Walter

Author's Note

MY INTEREST IN the remarkable *nisei* soldiers of World War II was sparked in 1980 by an elective Hawaiian history college course at the University of Hawaii. "What an amazing human drama of honor and endurance," I thought. Up to that point, my knowledge of their experiences and heroism was gleaned from occasional stories in newspapers and magazines. The course inspired what later became a series of magazine articles and, now, a book. It also provoked numerous questions, particularly about the effects of racism.

How did the *nisei*, the American-born children of immigrant Japanese, the *issei*, cope with the harsh inequities of the era? What were the racial dynamics between and among Asians, blacks and *haoles* (whites), especially on the Mainland? What was it like to be an American soldier with an Asian face during World War II? And more.

Within the time and space allotted, I've attempted to answer some of the questions through the soldiers' thoughts, feelings and images they can never forget. Every effort was made to use terms that came naturally to the men in their conversations. *"Nisei"* and "Japanese American," for example, were utilized interchangeably. (While most of the soldiers were *nisei*, a few were *sansei*, or third generation.) They frequently used the Hawaiian word, *haole*, when referring to Caucasians, and "concentration camp" instead of "internment" or "relocation" camp. Said a veteran: "On our evacuation to those camps—how would you feel if you were put on a damn bus, losing everything? Unless you've been through it, you don't know. 'Internment' is a euphemism. It denies reality. We were in a concentration camp." Another veteran, who saw Nazi horrors in wartime Germany, agreed: "Concentration camps are different from the death camps we saw."

There were frustrating moments while writing this book. The amount of information collected was so voluminous, many stories rich with irony, humor and drama could not be included. There was, for example, the brilliant performance by the 442nd Regimental Combat Team, especially the 2nd Battalion, during its spring 1945 push into Italy. There was the secret training encounter of some 100th Infantry Battalion soldiers with attack dogs on a place called Cat Island, where the Army theorized that the animals could detect "Jap blood." (They couldn't.) And there were many other stories.

In spite of numerous interviews and years of collecting data, only a small slice of the *nisei* experience can be related here. This "small slice" is an attempt to understand what the men and their families went through during the war. Because many voices are missing, this book can never do justice to the full depth of their sacrifices, emotions and experiences.

14

The boys of I Company at Camp Shelby: (Kneeling L-R) Henry "Bruno" Yamada, Tommy Umeda, Nobo Ikuta, Kazu Takekawa. (Standing L-R) Futao Terashima, Norman Yokoyama, Isamu Tando, Harold Watase, Jimmy Yamashita, Minoru Suzumoto, Edwin Naruse

Prologue

OME OF THE MOST COURAGEOUS SOLDIERS to emerge from World War II were Americans of Japanese ancestry. Through their eyes and voices, this book explores a few wartime connections and images the soldiers have never forgotten.

These connections with the French, Texans and Jews, to name a few, appear incongruous on the surface. However, a closer look reveals the thread that binds the seemingly disparate groups: Japanese American soldiers who were at once gentle liberators, fierce warriors and prisoners of war (in more ways than one) during a particularly difficult time in their lives. The French villagers of Bruyeres, for example, have honored the unusual-looking liberators for decades. Texans as well as many other Americans have never forgotten the rescuers of the Lost Battalion in France's Vosges mountains. Italians have memories of troops they sometimes called, "Chinese, Chinese." Only recently have people become aware of the soldiers' presence at Dachau, Germany. And even less is known about the experiences of Japanese Americans who were prisoners of war in Hitler's Germany.

Like the connections forged by these men, the wartime images they retain come in different textures and dimensions: the plantations of Hawaii, the farms of California, the family traditions of Japan; the racism that followed them and anyone else who looked Japanese during the war; the suspicion that dogged the men during basic training on the Mainland; the brutal battles they fought during and after the war.

Those battlefields and prison camps of World War II were far away in time and space when the veterans gathered at a summer 1990 reunion in Kona, Hawaii. Modest and unassuming, they did not fit the popular stereotype of soldiers commonly seen in John Wayne movies. When queried about their particular experiences in the war, most of the men echoed a similar thought: "When you come to my part, could you please say 'we' rather than 'I'? I was only one of many thousands. We were a team."

Camera crews were also present at the reunion, filming interviews with men who bore witness to a disturbing wartime sight as they moved with their unit through Germany—starving and dying Jews. The soldiers belonged to the 522nd Field Artillery Battalion of the 442nd Regimental Combat Team. Because some of them were present at two different but profound rescues—the Lost Battalion in France and the death camps of Dachau—many of their voices serve as a link throughout the book. At the risk of repetition, it must be emphasized that the voices are only a few of several thousand. Many will never be heard. They died a long time ago—unknown, unheralded. For every man who was interviewed, particularly for various battles, a hundred riflemen's voices were missing. Riflemen were always "point," taking the brunt of violence—land mines, enemy fire, shelling. That fact became painfully clear to this writer as the book progressed. One veteran pointed out the words on a coin, *E Pluribus Unum*—one of many. "I was only one of many," he said.

While the veterans shared their thoughts and feelings with filmmakers and writers, one of their number, George Ishihara, delighted us all by catching a 151-lb. *ahi* (yellowtail tuna) while fishing off the Kona coast. The fish was quickly turned into *sashimi* (the Japanese delicacy of fresh, raw fish) and shared with hundreds of fellow veterans, friends and relatives that evening.

It was an ages old cultural theme. Tired of their K or C rations during the war, the men often went to exceptional lengths to obtain fresh food—fish, chickens, cows, plants and whatever else they came across (an armadillo, in at least one instance).

Back then, these warriors aroused stares, questions and sometimes hostility because they were of Japanese ancestry—Americans caught in the double bind of racism and war when Japan attacked Pearl Harbor on December 7, 1941. In that tumultuous era, the men served in the U.S. Army's 100th Infantry Battalion, the 442nd Regimental Combat Team, the Military Intelligence Service (MIS) and the 1399th Engineer Construction Battalion.

The 100th and 442nd emerged from their European tour as the most decorated units of their size and duration in U.S. Army history. Japanese American soldiers with the MIS have been credited, albeit belatedly, with helping to shorten the war in the Pacific—from Alaska and Hawaii to China and Australia. Even before the outbreak of war, some Japanese Americans were sent by the U.S. Army's Corps of Intelligence Police (CIP) to the Philippines as undercover agents.

Thousands of miles away in Hawaii, meanwhile, Japanese Americans in the 1399th provided the hard labor required to build roads, bridges, airfields, runways, barracks and the like. Without them, the military and civilian communities would have had a difficult time. Yet, soldiers in the 1399th did their work under armed guard during the early part of the war.

Many of the Japanese American soldiers were studious and highly educated; like others of their generation, they were idealistic. And even though the men who were born and raised in Hawaii differed in practical and esoteric ways from their Mainland counterparts, *haole* and Asian, their lives would be forever intertwined.

Mainland-born Young Oak Kim, for instance, was a young lieutenant when he arrived at Camp Shelby, Mississippi in early 1943. The 100th, the majority of whom were Japanese American soldiers from Hawaii, had been moved to Shelby the month before from Camp McCoy, Wisconsin. Kim, who later became a much decorated soldier of the 100th, was stunned when he saw the men. "I was dumbfounded during that first week

with the 100th," said Kim with a smile in his voice. 'How come they can't speak English?' I wondered. 'They only speak pidgin to me to make my life miserable,' I thought. They said, 'Look at the 90-day wonder.' 'Look at the *kotonk* (slang for Mainland-born Asian).' 'Worse, he's a *yobo* (slang for Korean).'

"At first, I was surprised to see the Hawaii men with no haircuts, boots not laced, their shirts hanging out, but my only knowledge in OCS (Officer Candidate School) was that you judged combat ability on appearance—it was a standard inculcated in me. Once I got into combat with them, I learned the Army was all wrong. Nobody stays clean in a war. You have long hair and beards. You're messy, ragged and dirty. I learned appearances don't mean a thing."

Shining silver bars and polished boots meant virtually nothing where it really counted—in the field, in the mud and wet of foxholes, trying to stay alive. "That's where the rubber meets the road," said the 442nd's George Oiye. "You can talk about life at one level. But life is right where the rubber on your car is touching the road, taking all the bumps, taking all the crap that's down there."

The bumps were painful and numerous for the Japanese Americans. Some of the men were pilots, but they were routinely denied entrance into the Air Corps. Some discovered that their "friends" were no longer friends after December 7. Others, cleaning toilets during training, heard the word 'Jap' through barracks walls. Worse, some men saw their families torn by divorce or despair within the demeaning environment of concentration camps.

During a profoundly dark time when constitutional rights were denied their families, the soldiers responded with an untarnished record of valor. Without the excellence of the estimated 1,400 Japanese American men of the 100th who united under harsh, racist conditions in Hawaii, there might not have been a 442nd Regimental Combat Team. But there was a 442nd—more than 4,000 strong. The two units became a single "family" in Italy in June 1944, when the 100th became the first battalion of the 442nd Regimental Combat Team. So outstanding was the 100th's record, the battalion was allowed to keep its own designation.

Together, in Italy and France, the men of the 100th/442nd were a remarkable force, garnering eight Presidential Unit Citations and more than 18,000 individual decorations for bravery, including one Congressional Medal of Honor and 52 Distinguished Service Crosses. By war's end, about 33,000 Japanese Americans had served in the U.S. military.

Who were the men behind the medals? Their circumstances were so extraordinary, why do we know so little about them? Why haven't their stories been told much sooner?

Chronological events, dates and numbers, such as who was where when, provided only a small part of the complicated picture. Long untapped were the men's thoughts, feelings and other human facets of the war as they encountered one stressful situation after another. While specific dates, names and locations were often difficult to recall, the veterans could not forget certain images of the war. Only a few said they would rather not remember.

The men offered gentle warnings:

"War stories are bullshit."

"Be careful. So much time has passed. Different people will remember the same event differently, like *Rashomon*, the Akira Kurosawa movie. Sometimes, stories will be embellished and everyone will agree that's the way it happened."

"I need to know your intentions."

"Be careful reading our journals and citations. Some incidents are recorded incorrectly and don't tell the whole story."

"Are you going to whitewash certain events?"

"I've read the war books, and found parts to be true and other parts to be complete fabrication."

"War is war. You can't make judgments, only opinions."

"Talk to the foxhole soldier and get his private, personal war. Get my version, then get the version of the man 100 yards up the road, then you're getting a truer picture—two different slants on the same thing."

Unlike other soldiers who returned to hometowns singly and anonymously, able to tell stories without anyone to verify or deny them, the Japanese Americans generally returned as a tightly knit group to island or Mainland communities. They could not escape their wartime conduct for long. For the most part, this writer found the soldiers tended to give others the credit for courageous acts. "One of many," they kept repeating. "I was only one of many."

Kim expressed a cautionary thought on the subject of war. He remembered Italy and a young German soldier, about 18 years of age, who was badly wounded. "We cut away his trousers and tried to stop the blood flow, but we soon realized he was going to die. We were too far from the aid station, and there was no way to save his life. He tried to tell us something in German but we couldn't understand. By arm and hand motion, we gathered he wanted us to take out his wallet, which we did. And then he wanted us to take out some pictures. By his facial expressions, by his tears, we knew somehow that he wanted us to tell his mother about his last moments on this earth. And that, I think, hit us very deeply. We realized very very vividly that he was another human being—young, innocent, who meant no real harm to us, other than he was in the same bind we were … War is as close to hell on earth as man can create, and why people fight them, if you've ever been in one, you never understand."

From a distance of nearly 50 years, the veterans spoke of that "hell on earth" with various voices and perspectives. Many were philosophical. Others were matter-of-fact. Some were angry, expressing long held feelings. Most spoke candidly.

"We've been criticized for the fact that the Japanese Americans haven't told certain things, and I think that's a wrong criticism because it isn't that we haven't told, it's just that people weren't ready to hear it," said Oiye. "I'm absolutely sure of that. And right now, they're ready to hear it, they want to know. And because they're asking questions, we're giving answers."

(Upper left) George Oiye, 522nd Field Artillery Battalion. (Upper right) Medic, 100th Battalion. (Lower left) Duty in the Maritime Alps, Winter 1944-45. (Lower right) Jimmy Tatsuda, K Company, 3rd Battalion. Maritime Alps, Winter 1944-45.

PART ONE

Go for Broke

Soldiers

When I volunteered from Hawaii, I was prepared not to come back—there was no consideration of returning alive. If you make, *you* make*. *Not recklessly, but just do the best you can. You go for broke.*

George Ikinaga
442nd Regimental Combat Team

THEY WERE IN THE SEVENTH ARMY'S SECTOR in northeastern France—the Vosges Mountains, a chain of dark, dense and wet forests, about 100 miles in length and averaging 3,000 feet in height. It was October 1944.

Japanese American soldiers of the 100th Infantry Battalion/442nd Regimental Combat Team had just arrived from the hills of Italy, where they spent months fighting Germany's tough Wehrmacht units. When the 100th/442nd role with the Fifth Army in the Rome-Arno campaign was over, the outfit counted nearly 1,300 casualties—more than one-fourth of its approximate troop strength of 4,000. Behind the grim statistics were sons, brothers and fathers, many of whom were youths of 19 and 20 who volunteered from U.S. concentration camps. The surviving soldiers were emotionally strained, physically exhausted and shivering from the unusual cold. They needed to rest.

In the Vosges, however, the Japanese Americans stood at the last natural barrier between France and Germany. The forests' rough landscape of steep ridges arched around fertile valleys tended by a few families who farmed the rich topsoil and lived in small villages—Bruyeres, Belmont, La Broquaine, Biffontaine, La Houssiere.

In this pastoral setting, members of the French underground worked secretly for liberation from the Germans who had controlled the area since June 1940. "My father, Max Henri Moulin, headed the resistance," said Pierre Moulin, born in 1948. "From Bruyeres, he'd cross the line, risking his life to give maps and other information to the Americans."

The tide was shifting. Germany suffered a number of defeats by October 1944, including a retreat northward from the beaches of the Riviera and through the Rhone

---

*Hawaiian term meaning "die," pronounced "mah kay." The word may be found in *Hawaiian Dictionary* by Mary Kawena Pukui and Samuel H. Elbert.

Valley. But here, on the border so close to their homeland, the Germans were fired with a do-or-die determination. Firmly dug in, German troops would not easily give up their control of the fields and the thick pine forests of the Vosges, where the wind blowing through the trees makes a wailing sound. "All those pine trees," said Robert Tanna, G Company, 2nd Battalion. "All those gloomy days."

Troops of the 100th/442nd were attached to the 36th Division on October 13. Commanded by Major General John Dahlquist, the division was ordered to break the German entrenchment. (Originally a Texas National Guard outfit, the 36th suffered heavy casualties and was gradually filled with other replacements.) Up to that point, no known army in history had been able to breach the Vosges by force.

The division commander wasted no time in using the battle-tested Japanese Americans: the men took the neighboring villages of Bruyeres and Biffontaine by October 25.

Little more than 10 days before, the soldiers were facing Buyeres, dominated by four enemy-held hills (named simply A, B, C and D) which arched above the town and its vital transportation links—a railroad and three major roads. One of the roads led northeast through St. Die to Strasbourg, an objective of the 36th Division. The area was also a bastion of superior German firepower: heavy artillery; machine guns, well-hidden under the heavy underbrush of the forest; mine fields; booby traps; snipers; mortar fire and "screeming meemies"—six-barrel rocket launchers which emitted shrieking, nerve-wracking sounds. "It sounded like the cries of a hysterical person," said Walter Inouye, who belonged to the combat team's 522nd Field Artillery Battalion.

This was different from Italy. There, at least, the troops had some general idea of the enemy's location. But here in the dark forest, shrouded by rain and fog, the unseen enemy was everywhere. "The fog used to roll in by two in the afternoon," said Clarence Taba, I Company, 3rd Battalion. "It got dark early—very eerie. When traveling on a trail, you had to look at the sky for some reference point, peeking through the tall trees."

You could hear the Germans' tanks, but you couldn't see them, remembered Robert Sasaki, L Company, 3rd Battalion. "When things quieted down at night, we took turns at guard duty. I'd think about home sometimes, especially when the conversation turned to food."

It seemed their parents intuitively understood their sons' yearning for Asian food. "My father used to pack wooden boxes with rice, squid, abalone and send them to me once a week," said Susumu Ito, forward observer for the combat team's 522nd Field Artillery Battalion. "I felt sorry for the mailman because the boxes took up so much space in the mail bag."

Little wonder that the men missed fresh food. C rations, which came in a can, consisted of meat hash and crackers. K rations, packed in a waxed box, offered deviled ham, some cheese, dried coffee, cigarettes and a chocolate bar. "We'd burn the wax

Soldiers of the 2nd Battalion gaze at Bruyeres from Hill D.

around the box, which gave a nice clean flame, and heated our water with that," said Taketo Kawabata, G Company, 2nd Battalion. "But it was so gloomy in the forest, I wasn't hungry."

In the dreary setting, buried personnel mines, including non-metallic ones that escaped mine detectors, lay in wait for the men. "Bouncing Betties," for instance, exploded about five feet off the ground and showered a deadly umbrella of sharp steel that could kill, blind or amputate. ("Also known as nutcrackers," explained some veterans.)

"Tree bursts, those awful tree bursts," recalled the men. These were the most feared—sharp metal fragments that pierced the head and body with terrible force when shells hit treetops and exploded. "The shrapnel goes up, then you hear the fluttering," said Kawabata. "Then a hot burst hits you—so hot." Almost every shell fired by the Germans burst in the tall pines, raining steel on the men below. Slit trenches were useless unless they were protected by heavy logs. Realistically, there was no way the men could escape the deadly tree bursts. "You traded off one danger for another," said Chester Tanaka, K Company, 3rd Battalion. "If you ducked the tree bursts, you'd run into small arms fire."

Susumu Ito was impressed by Germany's advanced military technology. "Their 88-millimeter artillery were absolutely superior instruments and they were fast. See, you could always hear the sound of our guns before the shells flew. The Germans' artillery flew first and then you'd hear the gun go off. And their machine guns went brrrrp, ours went putt-putt-putt." (Forward observers like Ito moved with the infantry to direct artillery fire upon enemy positions.)

Another soldier, Neil Nagareda, described the impact of shells slamming their targets. "Close ones were like a train coming down a railroad track. Shells exploded and the mud and gravel fell on you. When the fragments passed, they sounded like fluttering … When you're under fire, everything seems sharper. Your hearing is so sharp you can hear all the gravel, you can see the mud fly by you. When the shells come, it sounds like bacon frying in hot fat—zzzzzzz. It's amazing."

Nevertheless, the Japanese Americans faced the barrage with an intensity that would rank them among the most decorated soldiers in U.S. military history. "When I volunteered from Hawaii, I was prepared not to come back—there was no consideration of returning alive," explained Hawaii-born George Ikinaga, a medic. "If you *make*, you *make*. Not recklessly, but just do the best you can. You go for broke."

Lieutenant Walter Matsumoto's 232nd Combat Engineer Company demonstrated this "Go For Broke" spirit. Among their duties, the engineers were responsible for clearing mines and opening up the roads so that jeeps, weapons carriers and trucks could keep the ever- advancing infantry supplied with vital necessities. (The 232nd was the only outfit within the 442nd made up entirely of *nisei* officers and men from the start.)

Matsumoto recalled one of the severest tests the engineers encountered at Bruyeres—the *abatis* (roadblocks), trees cut down by Germans and placed on roads and trails. "They'd post enemy snipers in case our men tried to clear the roads. We lost two men before we reached Bruyeres—Sergeant Abe Fujii, who was born on the Mainland, and Private Takeo Yamamoto, born on Oahu."

The fire came from four machine guns situated at a convenient vantage point on higher ground. The Germans concentrated their guns on the platoon, including Fujii and Yamamoto of the company's second platoon. "The terrain was pretty rough, with narrow roads, and the men were preparing to remove trees blocking the roadway," said Gilbert D. Kobatake, lieutenant, 2nd platoon. "We were told no Germans were in that spot. We didn't expect the Germans."

After the attack, the soldiers' morale plummeted; the sight of their dead and wounded friends was as shocking to their spirits and senses as the constant rain and cold—freezing, as far as the men were concerned. Just a few months before, the men baked in Italy's heat. Now, keeping warm and dry in the icebox atmosphere of the Vosges was almost impossible. "I got soaking wet in the woods later at Bruyeres when we camped along the railroad tracks," said Robert Sasaki. "We were in slit trenches

previously dug by the Germans. We were so tired that night, we fell asleep in the trench, half filled with water."

Their wet socks never dried out in their wet boots, recalled another soldier. "We tried putting the socks under our armpits to dry, but they never got really dry. The cold was so painful, it hurt my face … A hell, a horrible feeling."

Decades later, the miserable weather stuck out in the mind of Israel Yost, the 100th's chaplain. "Our forward aid station was a dugout with logs over the top, our feet in the water. I have definite memories of that."

The damp cold was especially hard on the men from Hawaii. Their teeth chattered, their eyes stung, their muscles shivered under the skin. For some, numb fingers and feet turned into swollen fingers and feet. For all, trench feet posed a constant threat—feet that turned purple, became swollen and, in the worst cases, needed to be amputated. Added to this hardship, the soldiers, an average 5′4″ in height, carried field packs that weighed 30 pounds or more.

They yearned for a hot bath, dry clothes and sleep. Some dreamed of *o furo*, the soothing, end-of-day Japanese custom of soaking in a wooden tub, the hot water warmed by a hand-tended fire beneath. Now, so far away, such images of home were far removed from the freezing cold and other life-and-death realities at Bruyeres.

"The (Germans) had to be cleaned out of four conical hills around Bruyeres," summarized Lawrence Nakatsuka in his 1946 book, *Hawaii's Own*. "The Germans … sent artillery shells crashing into the trees to score high casualties with tree bursts. Two days later, the 3rd Battalion took to the lines. Now three battalions plunged ahead under cover of a terrific barrage. Mortars, howitzers and tanks came to life in a drizzling rain as the 100th took Hill A and the 2nd captured another. The 3rd Battalion made a direct charge over 300 yards of open field for Bruyeres, occupying the town by nightfall. The 100th alone accounted for more than 100 prisoners. The two remaining hills fell soon after and the town was now secure."

Succinct though the summary, the taking of the hills was costly and complex. The 100th had waged a ferocious four-hour fight to take Hill A, the 2nd Battalion nearly seven hours to secure Hill B. Hill D fell to the 2nd Battalion on October 19, Hill C to the 100th on the 20th. The effort involved hundreds of soldiers.

The 100th's Captain Young Oak Kim harbored serious concerns about General Dahlquist's penchant for issuing "wrong information and crazy orders" and for not believing the warnings of others. In preparation for the last assault on Hill A, the 100th cut off communications to everyone at higher headquarters to avoid talking to Dahlquist, said Kim. "In the early morning at a forward outpost opposite Hill A, I got a phone call from Lieutenant Frank DeMaiolo, the communications officer, who said, 'Somebody wants to talk to you.' I asked, 'Is it who I think it is?' I pulled the line. Artillery had destroyed the other lines, so artillery could have destroyed this one as well. We couldn't attack just yet. We needed at least 25 minutes more. Dahlquist had insisted there was only a token number of Germans defending Hill A and that only our timid assaults prevented its capture. But we knew better from previous unsuccessful attempts. When the hill was taken, more than 100 Germans were captured and over 100 automatic weapons taken. We suffered only two wounded by attacking in our way on our own time schedule."

Kim, a Korean American, had been a young PFC with the Army when World War II broke out. In an era when the military generally viewed Asians as menial laborers, not soldiers, Kim became a rarity when he was sent to Officer Candidate School. But it appears the Army brass did not know what to do with his "visibility factor"—an Asian indistinguishable from other Asians when viewed through the military's eyes. He was sent to Camp Shelby, Mississippi in January 1943, where the 100th had been transferred from Camp McCoy, Wisconsin. By the time the 100th became a part of the 442nd at Civitavecchia, Italy in June 1944, Kim shone as a leader. The 100th evolved into a finely tuned instrument in Italy, especially when they were attached to the 34th Division, commanded by the highly regarded General Charles W. Ryder. France, however, presented the soldiers with a drastically different situation. "In Italy, the orders made sense," said Kim. "But here, in France, always crazy orders. We were not allowed to use our common sense …"

AS THE 100TH AND 2ND BATTALIONS made progress in the hills, the Germans started to withdraw from Bruyeres, said Robert Sasaki. "We ran across an exposed, open field to get to the town."

Robert Tanna, 2nd Battalion, watched as the soldiers made that run. "That was the highlight of Bruyeres—the 3rd Battalion coming into the open area. We were on the outskirts of Bruyeres and didn't know the 3rd was making the frontal attack. They made the attack through a smokescreen, a camouflage created when shells fired by the artillery exploded. Some Germans were still in the town."

A scout, Yoshio Iwamasa, was wounded that evening by a sniper, said Barney Hajiro, I Company, 3rd Battalion. "Iwamasa was about 100 yards ahead … I fired my BAR (Browning Automatic Rifle) at the building where I thought the bullets were coming from. Kazumi 'Portagee' Matsunami, my squad leader who used to watch over me, scolded me, 'You could get killed.'"

The Germans were relentless. Taketo Kawabata, 2nd Battalion, was in a farmhouse at Bruyeres when the enemy struck. "I think the Germans saw us moving around in the house and they fired their 88s. As soon as you hear the noise, the shell is right by you. The 88 hit the roof of the wooden building. The family was in the basement and shrapnel hit a little girl. She was wounded and crying."

It was at the farmhouse that Kawabata was reminded of another tragedy. "Before we got to that farmhouse, we were walking down the side of a road when we saw a guy lying on the side of the road. When we reached the farmhouse, this soldier, a *kotonk*, (Mainland-born Japanese) told me, 'You know, the guy lying down the road sure looked like my brother.' Ohhh, I felt so bad. How miserable he must have felt at seeing his brother blown up like that."

The soldiers darted from house to house, flushing out the Germans. Some I Company soldiers saw something odd in a house at Bruyeres. "We noticed some wire going into the basement and, sure enough, three Germans were sleeping down there," said Shiro Kashino.

Stan Akita remembered the moment Bruyeres was liberated. "The French were overjoyed (at seeing us). This is where we first witnessed the wrath of the French people on the collaborators. The male collaborators were beaten. The female collaborators were shaved bald and marched through town."

The sight left an uneasy impression on some of the soldiers. They witnessed poverty and desperation before in Italy, recognized the wartime stresses civilians had to bear and understood their rationale for doing whatever they had to do to survive. "People had to eat, they were hungry," said Sasaki. "It's easy to condemn. Who are we to judge?"

The villagers of the Vosges liked the Japanese American soldiers who quickly developed a reputation for their kindness, especially toward children. "They gave candies to my son, cigarettes to my husband and they paid me for the cabbages which

George Goto (standing far right) with buddies and French children at a wine-making section of Bruyeres. October 1944.

they took from my garden—they even asked permission to do that," said area resident Josephine Voirin in a 1979 interview with Lorene Nakamine, the daughter of a veteran. "I remember my husband shaking his head as he saw the soldiers charging in the open field from the forest and falling to the rifle and machine gun fire."

Memorials in the area today honor the soldiers not only for their sacrifices, but also for not repeating a historical pattern in war that could be traced to an earlier century when conquerors burned and plundered the villages. "Bruyeres is a place where the people remember old wounds, a place once overrun by German troops and others before who had wrought violence on the civilians—stealing, raping," said Chester Tanaka. "But they remember the soldiers of the 100th/442nd as gentle."

Frenchman Robert Giron documented his observations in a diary passage dated October 20, 1944: "Always very cloudy. Always Hawaiians. Very kind ... Many tanks ... We sleep in the cellar."

Another resident, Serge Carlesso, lost his left leg from an explosion during an intense shelling of Bruyeres in early October. His was an experience that illustrated the ironics of war. Wounded by American artillery, Carlesso was moved on a horse and cart to a hospital by German soldiers who risked their own lives by doing so. "Many Germans were also wounded, but the German surgeon operated on me first because my wounds were too serious," he recalled. "When the Americans came, they found me lying in the hospital cellar and evacuated me in an ambulance. There, I saw one 36th Division soldier and two Japanese Americans."

While sheltered at Bruyeres during the evening, the 100th was given orders at midnight to attack Hill C the next day. They had been promised two days of rest. "We planned and worked at feverish pace till 9 the next morning," said Kim. "Five minutes before 9, the Germans attacked the 100th's positions from where our own attack was to be launched. This required major last-minute changes, but the attack on Hill C began on time. Five minutes after 9, we breached enemy positions and captured 50 Germans ... The 100th completed the taking of Hill C. All this brilliant effort was negated when we were ordered by Dahlquist against our wishes to leave Hill C later that afternoon. Hill C had to be retaken by a battalion of the 7th Infantry Regiment of the 3rd Division at great cost."

Companies F and L of the 442nd's 2nd and 3rd battalions, respectively, had no rest either. Earlier, the combat team had been repulsed by a German stronghold at a railroad embankment east of Bruyeres. "We were at the edge of the woods, when we saw a high-ranking German officer walking by the railroad track," said James S. Oura, K Company, weapons platoon. "He looked toward our direction. We wondered if he saw us, but he kept on walking. We withheld fire. When the time came, we fired and he went down. When we got to him, we found some important maps and plans."

The documents proved crucial. F and L companies formed a task force commanded by Major Emmet L. O'Connor. The force sneaked through enemy lines at night, undetected. "We had some men wounded because the Germans were using the track to get us to expose ourselves by going over the embankment," said Harold Fukunaga. "We had to regroup there. That afternoon, I told the medic that my feet were getting discolored."

By then, the soldiers destroyed the enemy's resistance. "The task force killed 80 Germans and captured 56 prisoners," wrote Lawrence Nakatsuka in *Hawaii's Own.* "For this feat ... it was awarded the Presidential Unit Citation."

Pockets of Germans in the hills did not easily give up. The combat team learned that a strong German force of about 100 men had infiltrated Hill D again. Companies F, H and L were given the task of routing the Germans but the enemy was entrenched, with no intention of losing the hill a second time.

Technical Sergeant Abraham Ohama, waving a white flag, was hit on Hill D when he went to the aid of a wounded soldier from F Company. As litter bearers removed the wounded men, Ohama, lying helpless on a stretcher, was killed by enemy fire. Enraged and without a word, F Company troops rose to their feet, attacked enemy positions at close range and killed more than 80 Germans in the ensuing battle. Several Germans saved themselves by hiding and later surrendering. The episode illustrated the complexity of war—rage mixed with compassion.

Michio Takata remembered the charge and the "pitiful sight" that followed. "We devastated the Germans. By that time they were using boys—16 or 17-year-old kids. The Germans had run out of manpower. It was a pity to see young Germans yelling, getting shot and asking for mercy. It was pitiful. I remember our company commander, Captain Hill, trying to apply first aid to a 16-year-old whose testicles were blown away. A 16-year-old kid. I remember Captain Hill, with tears in his eyes, trying to help the boy. In the Vosges forests, you have the enemy in your sight, maybe 20 yards away. You can see him. If it had been the SS, I would have had no hesitation in pulling the trigger, but I saw 16 and 17-year-old kids in front, and it was not easy to pull that trigger."

Earlier that very morning, the same group of Germans had attacked a 2nd Battalion supply carrying party. In the fight to flush out the Germans, H Company's Staff Sergeant Robert H. Kuroda led a squad in an attack on a machine gun nest, made his way to within ten yards and killed the crew with hand grenades. When Kuroda noticed a 442nd officer was killed, he picked up the officer's tommy gun and hit another machine gun position. Kuroda was killed by a sniper. Takao Hedani, H Company, witnessed the incident. "We went to help the carrying party but we got pinned down too. Robert and I spoke briefly, after which I left him. About 50 yards away, he was hit in the throat."

The Kuroda Brothers: Ronald (left) served in the 100th. Robert, with the 442nd's 2nd Battalion, was killed in France, October 1944. Both received the Distinguished Service Cross.

Just two years before, Kuroda had been an electrician at the Aiea Sugar Plantation on Oahu. "After Pearl Harbor, Robert volunteered into the Army," said Joe, Kuroda's youngest brother. "In September 1941 I was attending Mid-Pacific Institute (a private high school) so Robert set aside part of his $21-a-month pay to help my parents with the expenses."

Kuroda, posthumously awarded the Distinguished Service Cross, was representative of many Japanese American families that had three, four, five, or six sons serving the U.S. during World War II. His parents, Toyoichi and Sekino Kuroda, had another son, Ronald, who served with the 100th's B Company. Ronald earned a Distinguished Service Cross. Still another son, Wallace, served with Hawaii's 1399th Engineer Construction Battalion, the U.S. Army's valuable and overworked labor force of Japanese Americans. Joe later served with the U.S. Army.

As in other wars, this one was loaded with irony. "We had four first cousins who were in the Japanese Army," said Joe. "One, a pilot, died over Singapore."

THE LIBERATION OF BRUYERES had come with a high price. But the blood was just beginning to flow. "Take Biffontaine," ordered General Dahlquist.

Kim was furious. Biffontaine, "a worthless tactical objective," was seven miles behind German lines. Despite vigorous objections, the 100th was forced to abandon the strategically sound position it held five miles behind German lines, putting the battalion beyond the range of friendly artillery support and radio communications. "The attack was finally made on Biffontaine after receiving several promises from Dahlquist, none of which materialized," said Kim. "We later had to fight our way back from Biffontaine. We took heavy casualties because in one day of fighting we were extremely low on ammunition, and in three days of fighting were without food and desperately needed medical supplies."

Of his Biffontaine experience, Stan Akita said, "I had a queer premonition that something was going to happen to me on October 23. I went up to Sergeant Saburo Ishitani and gave him my wristwatch and a beautiful rose gold German pocket watch which was to be sent home to my mother in case I didn't get back." (The items were sent to Akita's mother.)

It was still dark on the morning Akita went on detail duty, one of several guards assigned to take wounded men and German prisoners to the rear. Around 9 a.m., the tables turned drastically when the detail encountered a company of about 150 Germans, according to Akita's estimate. A few managed to escape, but most of the Japanese American soldiers became prisoners of war, destined for prison camps.

As the POWs headed toward an unknown fate, Biffontaine was taken. Strategically, the place was insignificant, a tiny cul-de-sac with no railroads or other vital military links. But the fighting for the hamlet was hand-to-hand, house-to-house, and cost the 100th

Battalion dearly. "We went into Biffontaine as the best unit in Europe, and came out with only one officer per rifle company and very depleted ranks," reflected Kim, whose hand was hit by machine gun fire during that action.

The overall toll on the soldiers of the 100th/442nd could be seen in a clearer light after Biffontaine: nearly half of their regiment of some 3,000 men were wounded or killed in or around the Vosges—this, within a few weeks of October.

Josephine Voirin's cottage, near the edge of the forest at Biffontaine, was crowded with dead or bleeding Japanese American soldiers. "Madame Voirin kept the bloody mattresses," said John Tsukano, 100th Battalion. "I saw the mattresses decades later, still soaked with their blood."

Israel Yost, who joined the 100th as chaplain during the Italian campaign, felt his anger rise as he knelt beside the broken bodies of his comrades. He and Katsumi "Doc" Kometani, a medical officer with the 100th, were frequently together. "Doc sometimes went out by himself, looking for the wounded," said Yost. "Once I worried because he hadn't returned all day. He told me later, he was pinned down by fire for hours."

Both men had seen inequities experienced by the 100th in Italy, many months before the unit became a battalion of the 442nd. "For me, a special person was Sergeant Kiyoshi "Jimmy" Shiramizu of the medics, who died of wounds in January 1944," said Yost of a man whose family was held in a U.S. concentration camp. "Jimmy was from California, one of the few kotonks in the early 100th. I agreed with him when he complained to me that the Army was wrong in not allowing him to put 'B' on his dogtags to show that he was Buddhist. That really riled me. When Jimmy was hit, he let the other wounded get help first, saying, 'I'm a medic, it's not right for me to go before the others.' We hadn't realized how badly he was hurt. There were no helicopters up in the mountains in those days to whisk him away to a hospital. Time was an element in his death."

Ten months later in France, as Yost and Kometani watched helplessly, the troops were pushed, pushed, pushed—annihilated in the forest.

Medics carry a wounded buddy to safety. Medics, too, died in the French forests.

The Lost Battalion

Our guys were shot up and we could hear them in the forest, crying out for their mothers. Even the Germans ... I could hear them crying in the darkness.

Barney Hajiro
I Company, 3rd Battalion

ON OCTOBER 27, THE DAY they were promised a break, the remaining soldiers were exhausted, physically and emotionally. "Everyone was so happy to be relieved," recalled Neil Nagareda. "It means you can take a shower. But no, it wasn't to be."

With barely a day of rest, General Dahlquist issued the 100th/442nd another order: "Rescue the Lost Battalion ..."

Two hundred seventy-five Texans, members of the 1st Battalion, 141st Regiment, 36th Infantry Division, were trapped on a steep ridge in the forest east of Biffontaine, cut off from the rest of their regiment and surrounded by Germans. The ridge began near Biffontaine and ended in a boomerang-shaped projection which protruded into the valley between Gerardmer and the town of St. Die.

"They were pushed so much by the general, who wanted to advance, advance, advance," remarked a member of the 232nd Combat Engineer Company. "Their battalion advanced so far, the men didn't have protection in the rear and they got isolated. The general had to get somebody to do the rescuing."

Others agreed the loss of a battalion posed serious ramifications.

How could anyone order a battalion to zoom ahead several miles into German territory without reasonable backup of any kind—communication lines, food, supplies, water, protection on the flanks? wondered many of the men.* "You're asking for it, you're asking for Germans to circle in and cut you off," said Chester Tanaka, K Company, 3rd Battalion. "It was a foolhardy military decision ... Two other battalions (of the 141st Regiment) were sent to rescue the men but they got beaten back. At the time we got word, we didn't know the details and were told to reach the Lost Battalion. They were low on

---

*Stories of the rescue are documented in the films *Yankee Samurai* by Katriel Schory and *Nisei Soldier* by Loni Ding, and in the books, *Unlikely Liberators* by Masayo Duus, *Go For Broke* by Chester Tanaka and *Bridge of Love* by John Tsukano.

food, water and ammo. Air drops were tried but the food and ammo got caught on trees or fell out of reach."

Lieutenant Walter Matsumoto, 232nd Combat Engineer Company, happened to be outside headquarters one morning when he heard the general berating Colonel Charles Pence, the regimental commander. "One thing I remember very clearly—the general of the 36th division (came) to headquarters and rode Colonel Pence, 'You got to get your men up there and push, push, push until you rescue the Lost Battalion.' And Pence is only a colonel. He can't say anything but, 'Yes sir, yes sir.' And I really felt for Pence because he felt so much for the boys."

At the start of the rescue, Susumu Ito was a "new" lieutenant. "Just prior to the Lost Battalion, I got a field commission at about 6:30 one morning when Lieutenant Colonel Baya Harrison called me up and said, 'Congratulations, Lieutenant Ito. Do you want to accept your commission?' I sort of gulped and asked, 'What's my commitment?' He said, 'Do the same thing you've been doing and you'll get $190 a month.' I thought, 'Wow!' Most enticing of all, we would get three days in a hot bath. We'd get to take a bath. Meantime, George Oiye got promoted to my staff sergeant position as chief of detail."

When Oiye got word about the Lost Battalion, he had just returned from serving with Lieutenant Al Binotti's forward observer party assigned to O'Connor's Task Force. "I thought I was going to get a shower, but didn't get a chance to change my wet clothes. I was immediately assigned to the Lost Battalion as an acting forward observer for K Company, since no other lieutenants were left."

Some, who could have stayed behind, volunteered for the perilous mission.

As an artilleryman, Francis Tsuzuki's view of the war had been relatively shielded. "A buddy, Richard Kurohara, admired the 100th and he was like me—he wanted to be more actively involved. Around midnight one night, Richard said, 'They're asking for volunteer forward observers.' I said, 'Fine.' Later we learned it was a battalion of the 36th Texas Division that was trapped ..."

Many soldiers, especially those from Hawaii, volunteered to go on forward observer missions where the chances of getting hurt or killed were much greater, reflected the Mainland-born Ito. "They'd come up to me and say, 'Lieutenant Ito, next time you go up, please take me, please take me.' They wanted to see what it was like. And basically that's what I wanted. I thought, 'If I'm going to fight a war I want to be in the thick of it.' And, not being cavalier about this, but my feeling was that if I were going to be shot or hit by a shell, that was my fate."

Ito's worried mother, interned in Arkansas, did not know the exact whereabouts of her son as he and hundreds of other Japanese Americans faced one of the most epic battles of World War II. She counseled Ito before he left for Europe, "Don't put yourself in danger—go to jail if necessary."

Everyone who could be mustered—indeed, it seemed everyone who could still walk, trench foot or not—was used for the rescue. The troops included the regiment's three battalions (the 100th, 2nd and 3rd), the 232nd Combat Engineer Company, medical detachment, the antitank, cannon and service companies and the 522nd Field Artillery Battalion. Members of the combat team's 206th Army Band were there. "Even the kitchen cook was up on the line," said Lizo Honma, Antitank Company, assigned to K Company, 3rd Battalion. "We also became part of the infantry."

ABOUT FOUR IN THE MORNING, October 27, the 100th and 3rd battalions moved into the pre-dawn blackness of the forest, treading through rain and slush into the abyss. Numerous hidden mines, tree bursts, cleverly concealed machine gun nests and everything else the Germans could marshal awaited the approaching soldiers. "We kept moving by holding each other's field pack (in front)," said Matsuji "Mutt" Sakumoto, I Company, 3rd Battalion. "We couldn't see beyond our outstretched arms."

It was so dark in the Vosges, attending to basic needs during the battle proved to be difficult. "When you got out of your foxhole to go to the bathroom and moved maybe a foot away, you couldn't find your foxhole again," said Eddie Ichiyama. "And you couldn't talk too loud, saying, 'Where's my foxhole?' Sounds carried. Being in the Vosges was like walking from sunshine into a pitch black theater. In October, it was dark and snowing already."

They moved with the 3rd Battalion—the central assault force heading toward the trapped Texans. The 3rd included three rifle companies (I, K and L) and one heavy weapons company (M). I and K Companies would suffer exceptionally heavy losses. Ito's team—Tsuzuki, Fred Oshima and radio operator Yuki Minaga—was attached to I Company, 3rd Battalion.

As the companies advanced, a scout ahead on the trail was wounded, remembered Ito. "And medics were called—medics started coming right away. But no one could get up, not with machine guns and tanks shooting at you. But you couldn't see them."

During an early stage of the rescue, Barney Hajiro fired his gun into the air. "I saw some soldiers from the 36th being chased by the Germans," said Hajiro. "This was October 27, when the Germans counterattacked ... I don't blame them for running, because the Germans had crack troops. The Germans were hitting what sounded like cans and that made a big noise—bang! bang! bang! I'm sure many others from I and K companies saw this. I think it was 'Portagee' Matsunami who told me to fire my BAR (Browning Automatic Rifle) in the air since we couldn't see the enemy. The Germans saw the smoke and fired a machine gun at me but I was behind a tree. They were confused. Soon after, we took off for a higher slope ..."

I Company had been given the left side of the road in the forest, said Matsuji "Mutt" Sakumoto, who belonged to the company's first platoon. "K Company was on our left and the 100th's B Company was on the right of the road, which I wasn't aware of at the time. We were informed the area ahead was all cleared by the 36th Division. We followed the ravine in the forest. Henry Nakada was point, I was second, about 10 yards, and behind me followed the company. I don't recall how far we walked when I looked behind and Captain Joe Byrne motioned to take a break … While on break, I leaned against a tree, lit a cigarette, looked up the ravine and thought, 'What a perfect spot for the Germans to fire.' After awhile, Captain Byrne motioned for us to move out. We didn't move out 20 yards when suddenly I heard a German yell, 'Achtung!' Then more jabbering. The Germans opened fire with their machine guns … I looked back, everybody hit the ground and it looked like the company was heavily hit. I later found out that when the German yelled "Achtung!" I Company's 3rd squad ran into a German machine gun nest. When the Germans fired, my friend Nobuo Amakawa was killed and the 3rd squad took a beating at that moment."

Mid-morning found I Company trapped in the ravine, pinned tight by German fire—machine guns interlocking their fire with other machine guns while mortars and grenadiers filled in the gaps. For Ito, the time in the ravine—"lying down on this damp, mossy soil"—seemed like eternity. "The radioman and two others had carbines and all I had was a pistol. And this German machine gun is shooting and it's kicking up, knocking leaves down, dirt flying all around you. I hear German voices: 'Hands up.' But you couldn't see them because we were in the midst of this thick pine forest."

Eventually, Ito's team made a mad dash up the other side of the ravine. "I believe we were pinned down for about three hours—couldn't move," said Tsuzuki, who was lugging a 40 to 50-pound battery. "Then our Lieutenant Sus Ito asked us whether we should make a run for it—go up the other slope. They say when you're scared you're not tired, but I tell you, halfway up the hill, I was tired."

Sakumoto recalled seeing some of "our guys" running toward higher ground. "Both Henry and I followed …"

As the soldiers neared the top, Tsuzuki heard General Dahlquist shouting at the 3rd Battalion's Colonel Alfred Pursall. "As I recall, he was with his aide, the son of Sinclair Lewis," said Tsuzuki. "And Dahlquist is yelling at Pursall, 'You'd better get those (trapped soldiers) out of there—rescue the boys!' Just like a football coach. All the colonel could say was, 'Yes sir.'"

There were many casualties that day, said Sakumoto. "Our 1st platoon must have been (hit hard), because we became the reserve, with the 2nd and 3rd platoons on the line. From there it was fighting all the way."

By now the battalions were fanned out—the 100th on the right flank, the 2nd on the left, the 3rd at the center.

K Company soldiers, at I Company's left, were moving along a ridge when a German tank and its infantry in the valley below stopped the men in their tracks. "We saw the tank coming down and you could see the muzzle pointing at us," said Satoru Sawai. What happened next happened quickly, as the tank fired its volley. "That's when I saw it, spotted the flash," said James Oura. "It was so hard to see in that forest, but you could hear the rumble of the tank."

The men scattered in various directions, seeking cover. "Joe Maeda was directly in front of my foxhole, and I remember having to keep my head down every time he fired his bazooka," said Tom Kawano. "He fired three shots and one finally hit the tank. I also remember our Pop Sano being hit." Another K Company soldier, 4th platoon, offered a perspective which essentially verified Kawano's observation. "Pop Sano, an old man of 38 who chewed cigars that were never lit, was on my left," said the soldier. "He popped out from the hole and started firing his M1 at the Germans emerging from the tank and at the infantry behind the tank. He did this, popping in and out of the hole. The third time he popped out, his helmet flew, and he was wounded."

The tank had been disabled by the fire from at least one known bazooka in the area, said another K Company soldier. "From my position, I also saw Joe Maeda in our (3rd platoon) shoot at the tank with his bazooka." That evening, the men could hear banging sounds—the Germans were repairing their tank. "Then they withdrew from the area," said Oura. "That's the last we saw of the tank."

Oiye, attached to K Company as an acting forward observer, remembered the blackness of night. He asked his captain, "Where's the enemy? Do you need a perimeter of fire?" The captain replied, "Right here. All around us. Just go dig a foxhole and wait for daylight."

Oiye and his team—Richard Kurohara, John Nishimura and Eddie Ichiyama—started digging foxholes but it was rocky and their efforts made a lot of noise. Suddenly, Oiye heard a different sound. "I said, 'John, what did you say? John, is that you?' I then heard a German voice, 'Kamerad.' I nearly jumped out of my skin. It was a German giving up. He could have slit my throat, but he came towards me with his hands up, waving a white handkerchief. I took him to the command post. I didn't know the password and almost got shot by the (442nd) guard there, I don't know who. It was so dark and raining when I turned the prisoner over."

Lizo Honma remembered the dark and rainy evening when he was guarding the perimeter. "I almost shot a kotonk guy coming down the hill because he didn't know the password. He didn't say anything. But I didn't shoot. I took a chance."

THROUGHOUT THE RESCUE EFFORT, fear, cold and lack of sleep in the Vosges placed enormous stresses on the infantry. The fog hovering over the forest lent an eeriness to the life-and-death scenario unfolding before the troops. Countless hours of lying in foxholes and hearing the cries of their wounded friends had to be a horrific dream, not reality. "Guys were shot up and we could hear them in the forest crying out for their mothers," said Hajiro. "Even the Germans … I could hear them crying in the darkness."

It was as though the men, even when moving quickly, were part of slow motion movie scenes, acting out different roles as they approached the Lost Battalion: one of the men squats to relieve himself and is shot in the head, the bullet piercing his steel

Trucks await release from the deep mud of the Vosges area. October 1944.

helmet. Another raises his head to study the landscape and is killed instantly. A soldier awakens one morning, looks at a nearby foxhole and sees the bodies of friends hit by tree bursts the night before. Still another soldier is blown off his feet by the explosion of a shell. After the dust settles, he says, "Where am I?" He doesn't have a scratch. A machine gun fires upon some K Company men at a roadblock of piled ammunition, including a water-cooled machine gun captured by Germans from the 141st Regiment. A squad of I Company men are standing together when a German mortar lands dead center. ("All that moaning and groaning," remembered a soldier who had just left the spot to fetch some food.) There are many incidents like that.

In another episode, some men are startled to see the two stars of the division commander. "Dahlquist came walking by us in his shiny uniform, unaware of the Germans' proximity," said the 100th's Kanemi Kanazawa. "That's why the Germans started firing. We pulled him down."

Many soldiers were hurt or wounded when they were ordered by an officer to take a detail down to pick up supplies right away, said I Company's Shiro Kashino. "From 20 to 30 men of the 3rd Battalion were picked … and I heard the supply jeeps coming up the mountain and it was dark and so quiet, you could hear a pin drop. I turned to the officer and said, 'We can't go down now, because the Germans will hear the vehicle moving up and they'll barrage the road because they know the road like the back of their hand.' The officer insisted we go. I said, 'It won't hurt to wait a couple hours, then go down.' But he insisted. We went down and the Germans barraged us—oh God, almost half the people got hurt badly. This fellow Kokubon's leg was blown off. I had to carry him. It was unreal. But I knew the Germans would hit us. Later, I told the officer, 'This tragedy didn't have to happen.' I wasn't disobeying his order. I just said we should wait."

Incongruous, almost bizarre dramas later became vivid memories for the men. "At dusk, a German medic in his gray uniform and pot helmet came meandering down the road as if on a Sunday stroll, as if he owned the road," said Chester Tanaka. "He didn't know he was in our area. We tackled him, and sent him to the rear."

In the rear, Neil Nagareda stopped in his tracks. "I came across this German arm sticking out, (his body) half buried already. I don't think the Germans had time to retrieve their wounded."

Butterflies darted to and fro in the forest. "Sometimes the light streamed through the forest, lending the place an eerie glow," said John Tsukano, D Company, 100th Battalion. "In combat, you could see the butterflies. Sometimes you could hear the birds." Another remembered the freezing temperatures. "In the morning, so cold, gun barrels would freeze from the moisture inside and we had to piss in the barrel," he said.

Around the second or third day—Tanaka can't remember exactly because "everything was so chaotic, so many ferocious small battles going on"—he saw the Grave Registration Officer (GRO) trucks, filled with bodies, a common sight in the Vosges. "They were picking up men from the 36th Division and also some Buddhaheads."

Medics like Henry Hayashida were not spared. Hayashida died in the Vosges while his brother-in-law, Stanley Akita of the 100th, was riding in a boxcar headed for a German prison camp.

Litter bearers had a rough time getting casualties from the woods to the roads. Thick mud constantly bogged down trucks and vehicles designated for the injured men's journey to a hospital area. Like many others of the Antitank Company, Donald Nakamura served as an ammunition and litter bearer. For the exhausted Japanese American soldiers, the usually larger *haole* men, made heavier by soaked clothing, were especially difficult to carry. "Four of us were carrying this German soldier on a litter through the forest, and I was the shortest guy," said Nakamura, barely five feet tall. "I was on the right side. So the German is saying, 'Right side too low.' His head was almost like a coconut shell, exposed that way, so I thought he was dead. But he kept on complaining, 'Right side too low.'"

Under these extreme conditions, platoons of engineers worked around the clock in shifts, supporting the infantry, clearing roads, locating antitank and personnel mines, and building roads for support and supply trucks. "We didn't build bridges in the Vosges as we had in Italy, but during the rescue we built corduroy roads," said Walter Matsumoto. "The hills were damp—it rained all the time. When you got trucks over the dirt roads, the roads were chewed up in no time. So we'd cut these saplings—two to three inches in diameter—lay them close to each other across the road, put some soil on top, whatever we could find, and filled up the cracks. That way we could pass over."

Surrounded by minefields and enemy fire, the troops advanced tree-to-tree toward the Lost Battalion. "On the third day, a bunch of us were by this tree, when General Dahlquist showed up and asked us why we were sitting, doing nothing," said Mutt Sakumoto. "We told him, 'We're the reserve platoon.' He told us, 'Don't let the other boys do all the fighting—flank the enemy.' You know when a general tells you to do something, you do it. Just before we moved, some of us remarked about how cleanly dressed the general's aide (Wells Lewis) was, with his lieutenant's bar shining on his helmet … He was killed minutes after the general ordered us to flank the enemy."

Wells Lewis was hit in the head by machine gun fire, said the 100th's Henry Sakato, who offered his perspective: "As the last man in my (B) company I was situated at the top of the hill, while the rest were dug in further down. I could see the division commander looking at a map spread over the hood of a jeep. Then he and his party—Lewis and the 100th's Lieutenant Paul Froning—walked toward my direction. They were so close to me, I could almost touch them.

"The general asked me when I dug my hole and I replied, 'Yesterday, noon.' He wanted to know how long we were there. The general told our company commander, 'Tell the scouts to move out.' A scout waved his hand as if to say, 'No, it's not possible now.' But the general insisted the scout move out. So the scout moved a little and dove toward the protection of a tree. When he hit the ground, German machine guns opened fire. I ducked, laid flat. As I looked up, I could see the general—he and Lewis were on the reverse slope where you could see just their top half. They were waist-high visible to the Germans. The bullets were coming up the hill, running parallel to the ground. Bullets were hitting the leaves and the leaves fell into my foxhole. Bullets hit Lewis and he fell. The general hit the ground and crawled a little ways down the reverse slope, got up and left ... I remember Lewis' image—his tall image—that's what hit me first. The incident stuck to my mind because I later learned he was the son of Sinclair Lewis, the Nobel Prize-winning author, and I had read his books."

The general's presence in the forest was troublesome, said Kanemi Kanazawa of the 100th's C Company. "Any guy walking around draws fire."

THE 100TH AND 3RD BATTALIONS were moving along the ridge toward the Lost Battalion when they encountered a strong German force of about 100 men. The approaches were heavily mined and very narrow at this point. The 100th, on the right flank of the 3rd Battalion, had to make a wide sweep around a minefield; the 2nd, on the left rear flank, cleared out a hill: The 3rd was ordered to face the Germans.

After several frontal attacks failed to flush them out, the soldiers of I and K companies fixed bayonets and charged steadily up the slope. It was a suicide charge, with little chance of anyone emerging intact. "I and K companies went forward—there were no officers in front of us," said Barney Hajiro. "Goro Matsumoto, next to me, got killed. I was with Kash (Shiro Kashino), and a German sniper picked him off."

Private Hajiro was one of the leaders of the charge who walked directly into the Germans' machine gun barrage, firing steadily as he moved forward. "Barney was one of the overlooked heroes," said John Tsukano. "The bullets kept going through him. To this day he has fingers like this (bent) but he just kept on charging, getting hit on the cheek, body, forearm. He should have gotten the Congressional Medal of Honor, but in those days it was rare for Buddhaheads to get that medal."*

Hajiro destroyed two machine-gun nests singlehandedly. When two snipers fired at him, he located and killed them. Hajiro, originally a messenger with M Company, happened to be at that deadly place because of a twist of fate.

The 100th/442nd was in Italy during the summer of 1944, when Hajiro witnessed

*Hajiro, recommended for a Congressional Medal of Honor, instead received a Distinguished Service Cross for his valor. However, an admiring British government honored the Japanese American in 1948 by awarding him the British Military Medal aboard the Canadian destroyer, *Cayuga*, at Honolulu Harbor.

Barney Hajiro is also honored by a decorated World War I Canadian pilot.

a street fight between an Italian civilian and a *nisei* soldier. "This is in enemy territory now—Italy was a fascist country at the time—and I jumped in to help the guy. It was a fist fight. I didn't want to see an American soldier get a licking. Because I helped, a Caucasian MP caught me, took me to my company, and I got a summary court martial. The Army taught us to kill or be killed, but not on the street. Next thing I knew, I was transferred to I Company where I didn't know anyone, and given a Browning Automatic, one of the most dangerous, powerful weapons of that time. I remember feeling real sad about leaving my friends in M Company. I was a messenger and Tadao Beppu, another Maui boy, was my platoon sergeant."

Hajiro made friends in I Company, many of whom were with him during that charge on October 29. There was Mainland-born Eiichi F. Haita, who used to carry Hajiro's 20 rounds of BAR ammunition. "Eiichi had a beard and didn't like to shave," recalled Hajiro. "Portagee Matsunami used to call him 'Mauldin,' after Bill Mauldin, the wartime cartoonist who had a beard."

There was Takeyasu Onaga, a bazooka man who used to take care of his fun-loving, beer-drinking friend, Barney. "I was a goof-off from M Company where I used to end up in KP all the time. Onaga kept me out of trouble."

He also used to check and load Hajiro's BAR. "Onaga looked sad that day," said Hajiro. "He knew the battle was going to be rough, that you cannot get up. Once you got up the Germans shot you because they were waiting."

German guns usually found their mark. "Snipers were getting our guys in the forehead," said Joe Shimamura, K Company. "They must have had a telescopic rifle. This is why nobody wanted to get up."

Nevertheless, the riflemen rose to their feet, charging and falling in great numbers. German machine guns rained fire on the men wherever they moved. "I thought I had it at that time because I felt bullets hitting the ground beside me," said Matsumoto. "I happened to look at the right of me and got a glimpse of something falling from a tree and it exploded right on top of one of our men—a German potato masher. At that very moment, the guys from our 2nd and 3rd platoons kept yelling at us to move. I guess it gave us the extra something and we all charged. Was I surprised when we came upon the German machine gunner—he was just 10 feet in front of us. We ended up right on the road with some of the 2nd and 3rd platoon guys. In front of us, not more than 15 yards away was a German tank slowly moving backward. We yelled for the bazooka man, and Onaga came running down the hill, his hand grasping his neck, his other hand toward us. The medic standing by us told Onaga to lie down. The next minute he was dead, shot in the neck. That was the last we saw of the German tank."

During the assault, bullets slammed into Hajiro's left side—his cheek, shoulder and forearm. At some point, his weapon flew. "I was stunned—I couldn't find my BAR," said Hajiro. "I heard the medic telling me to get down. The medic didn't want to stand up.

Me, I was stunned already. I didn't care for life already. At that time I didn't care … All that blood. I was disgusted with life. I walked back. I remember seeing Colonel Pursall by a tree with a pistol in his hand. I told him, 'Let's go up.' Then the medic pulled me down."

Joe Shimamura distinctly remembered Pursall—"I was hugging the ground, looked up and was startled to see him"—and the charge. "Masuichi Yogi got killed in front of me during the charge. Also James Okamoto and Fred Ogata. When I ran out of ammunition for my sub-machine gun, I remembered where Okamoto was and went back to get his rifle. He had been shot in the temple."

The enemy fired directly at wave after wave of attacking troops, killing and wounding many. "A guy in front of me, Wallace Ogata, was pinned down. Nobody moved since the snipers were picking us off," said Shimamura. "I heard a loud noise, like a bullet hitting a helmet. I saw Wally's head go down. I yelled, 'Wally!' I thought he was dead. He looked up and shook his head. The impact of the bullet on his helmet knocked him out. But he was alive."

Francis Tsuzuki also saw Pursall with a pistol in his hand. "He was telling everybody to charge, the so-called *banzai* charge. Hey, I'm an artilleryman. I don't have to charge, but like a damn fool, I charged up the hill. You couldn't see the Germans, you could only hear the loud fireworks, like New Year's Day."

Richard Kurohara remembered the incident in a similar way. "Pursall said, 'Infantry, attach bayonets.' And me, in the artillery, with only a .45, a toy pistol. So I figured I cannot attack without an M1. I was by this rock and Pursall said, 'You artillery, you charge too.' It was Indian warfare, dodging bullets from tree to tree."

There are situations in which "you throw the book out the window," said Yuki Minaga, a radio operator with Lieutenant Ito's forward observer party. "Pursall said, 'The hill is almost taken—we need someone to lead.' I got up. I didn't want to, but that's how it came out. My concern was to die fast, not get wounded. I had heard friends crying …"

There were numerous such occasions in which the soldiers thought they or their friends were about to die. "We were in the rear, when a 37 millimeter shell stopped right between my legs," said Ichiyama, a forward observer . "I said to myself, 'Ichiyama, this is it.' Then I heard someone say, 'Run, run, run!' and I ran. Luckily, it happened to be a dud."

As far as Neil Nagareda is concerned, there were many other unknown soldiers in the Vosges. Once he remembered standing at a clearing in the rear when it was hit by German shells. "Out of the 12, three were duds. It showed me some unsung heroes of the war were prisoners who were working in an ammunition plant somewhere. I don't know what kind of prisoners, but they must have been sabotaging the ammunition. The prisoners were taking a big chance, because they'd be shot dead if they got caught."

THE GERMAN TROOPS were an immovable force at the outset; after the charge by the 100th/442nd, remnants of their force fled in disarray. But the damage to both sides was severe. The battles lasted from morning till the afternoon, recalled Sakumoto. "Man, did we take a beating that day."

The men who followed saw foxholes with dead Germans. "Some Germans had bottles of whiskey, schnaps, or something like that," said an I Company rifleman. "We were told not to drink it—might be poisoned."

Tsuzuki cannot forget the sight that greeted him."Oh God, so many of our guys wounded or killed. I remember the Germans too, the wounded who cried out, 'Vasa, vasa'—water, water. What can you do? We had our own wounded to care for. We couldn't wander off."

It would have been deadly for the soldiers to stop, since deviating even a few feet could lead to mines. "We followed a trail marked with toilet paper, left by whoever cleared the minefield," said Tsuzuki. "So either way you can't do anything."

About three-fourths up the hill, Kurohara and Tsuzuki came upon a foxhole. "Two German soldiers were there—one dead, the other a mortally wounded officer," said Kurohara. "Francis commanded the officer to turn over his gun belt. The German died soon after … Action was taking place so fast and it was so noisy."

Tsuzuki remembered something else about the German officer. "He was in a beautiful foxhole—they had the time to dig these nice foxholes. A medic was going to remove him to attend to his injuries but the German refused. He may have known he was going to die. He looked up at me and smiled, 'Nein, nein.' He actually smiled at me. I can't forget that."

The fighting was so ferocious, there were no American officers left either, said Ito. "I remember three, I think, then there were none … Incredible."

The engineers were busily clearing mines several hours before the troops finally made contact with the Lost Battalion the next day. "They were clearing a road when a mine went off and an engineer fell down," said K Company's Tom Kawano. "He got up, shook the dirt off and kept on working. We couldn't believe our eyes."

The unknown engineer was one of many. "We got shelled many times but we had to do our work," said Gilbert Kobatake. He remembered the day clearly because shrapnel pierced his back at about the same moment Captain Joe Byrne was killed.

Byrne, highly respected by the Japanese American troops, was known for his calm nature and thoughtfulness. He remembered and correctly pronounced the unusual names of his men, something most *haole* officers did with difficulty. "Byrne knew the Hawaii boys from the time he was stationed at Schofield Barracks on Oahu," said I Company's Minoru Suzumoto. "Byrne stuck by us all the way. He was a classy guy."

Before the incident that took Byrne's life, Kobatake experienced another significant

I Company Pals: Kazumi "Portagee" Matsunami (left) and Shiro "Kash" Kashino at Camp Shelby, Mississippi.

event that day which was directly related to the tall, lanky I Company commander. While working, Kobatake saw another Japanese American walking ahead, a sergeant whose name he did not know at the time. Kobatake joined the sergeant. "I said, 'Why do you go ahead by yourself?' He said he was recovering from flesh wounds (at the aid station) when he ran away to rejoin I Company. As we talked, the shelling came. It got so bad at one point we had to take cover. After the shelling I didn't see the sergeant."

Later that day, the engineers were clearing the mines when Byrne saw them, according to Kobatake. Bryne was accompanied by officers of the 100th. Kobatake advised Byrne to follow a safer track through the woods. "But another officer said, 'No, our sector is on the right side of the road.' I again said, 'No, it's better to take this trail.' He said 'No, we'll stick to the right.' I should have forced them to take the safe trail."

Kobatake went ahead of them, Bryne following, when a Bouncing Bettie exploded between the two men. "Byrne was next to me, breathing but hurt badly and gurgling blood. I didn't know it was Byrne at the time—I'm an engineer, he was in the infantry. An aid man came to me. I said, 'Take care of him.' But the aid man said, 'He's too far gone.' I said, 'Who was he?' The aid man said, 'Captain Byrne.'"

Kobatake's back was so badly injured he couldn't walk. He saw their jeep. "I told them to put me on the front of the hood (for the journey) to the aid station."

It was already dark when the ambulance arrived at the station around six that evening for the trip to the hospital. "When they placed me in the ambulance, whom did I see but that sergeant—I learned his name was Kashino—I walked with earlier. He had been wounded in the leg about noon that day. I told him about Captain Byrne. He replied, 'I left the aid station the first time to rejoin my unit because of Captain Byrne.'"

Such actions by wounded *nisei* soldiers—leaving aid stations or hospitals, rejoining their buddies at the front and getting wounded again—were apparently well known. "Shiro Kashino was the greatest soldier I ever saw," said Barney Hajiro, himself a candidate for the Congressional Medal of Honor. "Kash got wounded six times, received six Purple Hearts. That's a record. When wounded, he still returned to his unit. The 100th had Captain Kim, we had our Shiro Kashino. We looked up to them."

The drive of the 100th/442nd, the thought that they wanted to get us out of that hill, sticks out in my mind. They suffered to get in there, oh, they suffered a lot ...

Harry McGowan
1st Battalion, "The Lost Battalion"

WITH SO MANY SOLDIERS killed or wounded, despair in the forest was as thick as the tangled underbrush. A company usually held about 180 to 200 soldiers; more than half in each company were already killed or wounded by the dawn of October 30, before contact with the Lost Battalion. Though their ranks were thin, the soldiers courageously edged ever closer to the Lost Battalion.

Courage was also found in the foxholes of the Lost Battalion. Trapped for a week under intense pressure, rising casualties and the pounding of artillery, the soldiers stood their ground. "There was no moving around in the daytime, only at night did we get water," said Harry McGowan. "We were using the same water hole as the Germans, so we took turns filling each other's canteens. We had some nourishment from the candy bars the artillery fired in to us."

Fear and apprehension set in, recalled Buck Glover, one of the few survivors of the Rapido River crossing in Italy, where the 36th suffered heavy loss of life. "We wondered, 'Will they be able to come and get us? When are they going to come?' These questions came popping up. After several days, we realized we weren't going to get any food, any ammunition, any water. When planes finally flew over, the first case of rations they dropped hit one of our men on the head, broke his neck and killed him ... You see your buddies getting killed and you place things in perspective. I was already feeling like a fugitive from the law of averages."

The men were also running out of hope. "We felt our chances of coming out of it were practically nil unless somebody broke through," said Harry McGowan. "We didn't know who at the time."

Resistance was faltering, but the 100th/442nd still lost men to enemy fire. "I didn't know where I Company was, I didn't know where anybody was, I didn't know my front from my rear because of the confusion," said a K Company soldier.

As casualties rose, strong feelings were expressed in a letter from the 3rd Battalion's Chaplain Masao Yamada to Colonel Sherwood Dixon, a staff member of the War Department in Washington. It was dated October 30, 1944: "After four days, we are

Chaplains of the 100th/442nd. (L-R), Hiro Higuchi, 2nd Battalion;
Israel Yost, 100th Battalion; Masao Yamada, 3rd Battalion.

still pushing to get through … The Major General is quite concerned and has commanded the 442nd to push … The cost has been high … Our men take their orders in stride without complaint and go into the volley of fire with one spirit, one mind. Actually, those who saw the charge came home with a vivid and stirring account of our men unflinchingly charging on the double, falling under machine gun fire, yet moving on as the ceaseless waves beating on a sea shore. I am spiritually low for once. My heart weeps for our men … I am probably getting too soft, but to me the price is too costly for our men. I feel this way more because the burden is laid on the combat team when the rest of the 141st is not forced to take the same responsibility … When we complete this mission, we will have written with our own blood another chapter in the story of our adventures in Democracy." (Yamada was seriously injured about a month before in a mine blast in Italy which killed three others in his jeep. Though weak, he accompanied his men to France.)

Soldiers of the 100th/442nd made contact with the Lost Battalion by the late afternoon of October 30. "Between 1500 and 1600 hours, the 3rd and 100th battalions entered the area of the First Battalion of the 141st," wrote Chaplain Yamada in a letter to Colonel Harrison Gerhardt dated October 31, 1944. "When those who pushed met the once-trapped troops, their efforts seemed all worthwhile."

I Company's Sergeant Tak Senzaki and Mutt Sakumoto were among the first to reach the Lost Battalion. Sakumoto described the encounter: "Henry Nakada was the point, I was second and the rest of the company behind us. Henry was about 10 feet away on the side of me as we went from tree to tree … I could see in a distance one or two persons moving about but when I told Henry and Sergeant Senzaki, they didn't see any movement. The next time I looked ahead, I saw this GI look straight in my direction. I

Relieved soldiers emerging from the forest, after
the Lost Battalion rescue.

kept looking and looking until he motioned to his buddies. Then everybody started yelling and motioning to come ahead. I was taken directly to their command post where I met a lieutenant—I forgot his name—who introduced himself as the commanding officer. We talked for a while, he asked my name, and promised me something which I forgot. The 'Lost Battalion' was dug in on a slight hill, the command post in the center. I Company took over the defense of the perimeter."

The Fighting 36th, a book about the 36th Division, described one facet of the encounter: "Sergeant Edward Guy, New York City, was on outpost when he saw somebody. He strained his eyes looking and then he raced down the hill like crazy, yelling and laughing and grabbing the soldier and hugging. PFC Mutt Sakumoto just looked at him … and the first thing he could think of to say was, 'Do you guys need any cigarettes?'"

Other I Company men in the back recalled watching Sakumoto for the "all clear" signal. "When he gave his okay, the rest of us followed," said Clarence Taba. "I remember seeing the Lost Battalion but we couldn't stop. We were given instructions to go on to the next hill. At that point, there were maybe 15 or 20 of us left, including our weapons platoon."

Meanwhile, Oiye's group managed to survive a trap laid earlier by the Germans and finally saw the men of the Lost Battalion. "It was an unbelievable sight," he recalled.

At least 20 men of the trapped battalion were wounded, their medics keeping watch over them, wrote Chaplain Yamada. "Two or three of the wounded died during that (stranded) period. Trench foot also set in, and many more were incapacitated by swollen feet. In all, about 70 were under medical care during their trying period."

Two hundred eleven men of the 1st Battalion eventually popped out of their foxholes, ecstatic, their gaunt faces expressing the relief. "We were so happy, everybody threw their weapons down and ran to each other, just hugging each other, saying, 'God, thank you, thank you, thank you,'" said Harry McGowan. "I can't describe the feeling—it was so highly charged."

The Japanese Americans were the most pleasing sight in the world to Buck Glover. "I saw this short, dark-skinned kid come up, wearing an American helmet several sizes too big. Did that matter? No. Here was a brother of mine coming up to save my life … As long as I live, I will never forget the soldier who asked, 'Are you guys out of cigarettes?'"

The meeting of the Japanese Americans with the doughboys of the first battalion was a touching moment, wrote Chaplain Yamada. "They smiled heartily at the Japanese Americans and for a moment forgot the ugliness of war. Many shook hands and said, 'If it weren't for you, only God knows what would have happened to us.'"

The soldiers of the Lost Battalion were resilient and strong, said Chester Tanaka of troops who had been ordered into their untenable situation. "They had to stay in one spot for a week. Surrounded by Germans, they couldn't move. The Germans directed every

The infantrymen could dodge bullets but they could not escape the mud and freezing cold of Bruyeres. "It rained constantly," was a common refrain.

kind of fire at them. It's amazing they survived. They said we came just in time ..."

When Tsuzuki reached the area, he noticed bodies of German troops around the perimeter of the foxholes. I asked one guy, 'Hey, what happened here.' He replied, 'The Germans couldn't get out during the day so they infiltrated at night.'"

Said Tom Kawano, "One of the rescued men told me, 'I hope the brass learned a lot.'"

The danger was not over. Shortly after the rescue, Tadao Beppu, an M Company survivor, was lying in a foxhole when he was struck in the leg by a tree burst. "The medic says to me, 'You may be the last we'll pull out because we're going to take first the ones with chest and stomach wounds,'" said Beppu, whose shin bone was shattered. "I said, 'Go ahead.'"

Like Beppu, Richard Kurohara spent some time shivering in a foxhole after the rescue. "After we dug for in the night—it was a foxhole large enough for two people— I covered myself with chopped branches, leaves, stones and dirt for protection from the tree bursts. We told another soldier to dig in too. He may have been exhausted because he did not. The last I saw, he was leaning against a rock. Next morning, he was dead—shrapnel in his chest."

Officers were rare by now, said Clarence Taba, I Company. He remembered going to battalion headquarters and saying, "No officers, send us some." The colonel replied, "Three lieutenants are on their way." The infantry lieutenants never made it to the top. They had been injured. Meanwhile, Taba's captain was killed. "So I told this first lieutenant, 'You're now the company commander.' But he said, 'I'm the executive officer, I'm not in command.' I went to Colonel Pursall and said, 'He refused to take command and ought to be court martialed.' But Pursall said, 'I'll commission you and you take over.' Because I wasn't trained as an officer, I also refused to be commissioned as a lieutenant. But Pursall made me a first sergeant. That lieutenant actually refused to be put in charge. He may have been shell shocked because he was eventually evacuated to the hospital. So I ended up as acting company commander—me, a clerk."

The exhausted infantrymen were pushed further the next day. I and K companies were virtually decimated but the new order from the division commander was to run the enemy off the ridge entirely. Again, the combat team was in control after a fierce battle. Again, a new order: move the enemy off the forward slope of the ridge to the valley floor at St. Die. "There was a lot of enemy resistance," said Lizo Honma. "Even after the rescue, many more men got killed."

The men were under extreme stress from having to do the virtually impossible. How much more could any human being bear? "Sometimes you're so numb from war, you're not human already," said Taketo Kawabata. "You think, 'Am I going to be the next one?' because every day your friends got killed."

Every human being has a breaking point, said the men. "See, after the Lost Battalion rescue, we pressed on for two more weeks and at the very end, we wished we would have some minor injury so we could go back," recalled Eiji Suyama, K Company. "At the end, there were only 17 of us left."

Problems still plagued the few who survived the ordeal. "I had trench foot," said Robert Sasaki, L Company. "One morning I took my shoes off and couldn't put them back on."

TROOPS OF THE 100TH/442ND lined up for review on November 12. General Dahlquist wanted to extend his personal thanks for their accomplishments, but there was virtually no one left to honor. Only eight riflemen from I Company stood at attention. K Company had 17 men remaining. (K Company earned seven Distinguished Service Crosses during the war.) There were 11 men standing from B Company. And so on. In all, only a few hundred, rather than several thousand, stood in front of the division commander. When he asked, "Where are the men?" Colonel Virgil Miller, the regimental executive officer, replied, "That's all that's left."

Within a month of fighting—from Bruyeres to St. Die—the 100th/442nd lost about two-thirds of its men. Casualties were estimated at 2,200, including 161 dead and 1,800 in hospitals. For the Lost Battalion ordeal alone, casualties suffered by the Japanese Americans were more than four times the number of men rescued.

The saga of the Lost Battalion was far from finished. More than forty years later, Lyn Crost, World War II correspondent for the *Honolulu Star-Bulletin*, came across information long unnoticed in the 442nd Infantry Journal. During the mission to save the Lost Battalion, Dahlquist had ordered the 522nd to fire upon a certain hill. Luckily, an officer questioned the order—"Isn't that right in the middle of the Lost Battalion?"—and radioed headquarters for more details. "Yes, it's in the middle of the Lost Battalion," replied headquarters.

For Kim, memories of France "still show the bitterness burnt deeply into my soul." In a 1982 keynote address to his wartime buddies at the 100th Infantry Battalion's 40th anniversary gathering in Honolulu, Kim said, "Later, Gordon Singles (the 100th Battalion's commander), while filling a brigadier general's position at Fort Bragg, refused to publicly shake General Dahlquist's hand at a full dress review in the presence of the entire III Corps. Dahlquist was then a visiting four-star general. Singles preferred remaining a colonel than to shake Dahlquist's hand ... Years after he retired, General Pence (the 442nd commander) could not mention Dahlquist's name without his voice shaking with anger."

Decades later, some of the men's voices trembled with emotion, while others were low key and matter-of-fact when they spoke not only of their time in the Vosges but also of their wartime experiences in general. Their opinions were varied. "War is war." "We were a unified fighting outfit—we did what we had to do." "We were expendable." "A few higher ups were reckless." "Sure, the 442nd was a good, crack outfit, but why use us every time? Why us every time?" "I volunteered to fight for my country." "The key was that we trusted each other like a brother." "You shed dry tears when you're old."

Ultimately, it was a matter of honor, said others.

Susumu Ito remembered an officer friend who admonished him when he embarked on the mission to reach the Lost Battalion. "He said, 'Goddamit Ito, why did you accept this commission? You could have been sitting back. Look what you got yourself into.' But I didn't then, nor do I now, ever regret it."

Said Tsuzuki of that last week in October: "The experience was nightmarish. I can never forget it."

Postscript

TIME HAS NOT FULLY ERASED the signatures left decades ago by nearly a month of intense fighting in the Vosges. Back then, the casualties suffered by the men of the 100th/442nd were not fully realized. With each passing decade, however, the ramifications of the incredible battle in the forest have become wider known and appreciated. Today, the Rescue of the Lost Battalion is considered an epic event, one of the most heroic battles of World War II.

The villagers and their descendants haven't forgotten the remarkable Japanese warriors. In the hills beyond Bruyeres stands a monument built by the townspeople in 1947 to honor the soldiers of the 100th/442nd who liberated their villages, showed kindness and died in the forest, far from their homes. Foxholes covered by weeds and tree trunks scarred by shrapnel remain silently in the darkness that shrouded so many soldiers in death years before. An old canteen lies in the underbrush. Engraved, "H. Hayashida," it belonged to a medic killed in the Vosges—Henry Hayashida.

Today, sunlight streams through the tops of the tall pines, trees once feared because of the deadly rain of steel. The filtered sunlight lends a cathedral effect to the setting, similar to the scene observed by a soldier during that terrible time in the forest. Butterflies still dart to and fro like they did when the soldiers came to fight so long ago.

And, just as before, the wind blowing through the trees makes a wailing sound.

PINEAPPLE FIELD NEAR HONOLULU, T. H.

PART TWO

Promises
and Perils

OR THE LIBERATORS, the drama that unfolded in the gloomy Vosges was not the first or last of its kind. Before the 100th Infantry Battalion became a part of the 442nd Regimental Combat Team in June 1944, the 100th lost numerous troops during the Italian campaigns of 1943-44. The Battle of Cassino, fought in the dead of winter, was a particularly brutal experience for troops of the 100th. Casualties were so heavy, Cassino would be forever known as Purple Heart Valley to these men. By the end of its tour in Italy, the battalion had little more than 500 men left. But many of the 100th's "Little Iron Men" who made it through Italy did not survive Bruyeres and the Vosges forest.

The troops of the 100th/442nd were remarkable liberators, men who aroused curiosity and questions wherever they went. They had Asian faces. Small in stature, wearing spectacles, many looked like mild-mannered schoolteachers. Most spoke a different kind of English called "pidgin."

The civilians knew the unusual looking soldiers as gentle, friendly men who shared their chocolates, cigarettes and food. When the men needed food, they paid for it. German soldiers and fellow American troops knew them as driven, extraordinary warriors who fought hard and obtained every given objective. "Why do you fight for America?" the Germans wanted to know. The civilians asked, "Where do you come from?"

A masterpiece by Usaku Teragawachi, one of the finest 20th century portrait photographers in Hawaii. The former laborer ventured into photography in 1913. When he died in 1964, he left behind thousands of exquisite photos that show the transition of a culture.

Hope

When I was growing up, schoolteachers told us, 'Forget your Japanese heritage—be American,' ... During my growing, society stressed this kind of thinking. But the history we learned had no bearing on my life— Pilgrims and stuff like that.

Walter Inouye
442nd Regimental Combat Team

THE SOLDIERS FROM HAWAII shared similar cultural experiences: the schools, farms, neighborhoods, temples, sugar plantations, ethnic foods and sports of the Hawaiian Islands.

Plantation ties were particularly strong on the Neighbor Islands. Barney Hajiro, one of the many remarkable soldiers of the Lost Battalion rescue, came from the plantation town of Puunene, Maui. So did his friend, John Tsukano, the soldier who observed and never forgot the bizarre image of butterflies and blood in the Vosges forest.

Family, marriage, school and work relationships among island soldiers were strong. The 100th's Goro Sumida was one of six brothers who served in the war. (By the time Sumida returned from the war, his mother's jet black hair had turned white.) Walter Matsumoto, a 232nd combat engineer, was one of three sons serving with the 442nd.

In contrast, the childhood communities and experiences of the soldiers from the Mainland were varied—from the farms of California and the fisheries of Alaska to the mining towns of Wyoming and the isolated mountain ranges of Montana. Susumu Ito, for instance, was born in Stockton, California. His parents, sharecroppers, also had a bathhouse business. "The Japanese there lived among other Japanese and the *haoles* lived in a different area so that being discriminated against was pretty much accepted, part of growing up," recalled Ito.

Washington-born George Ishihara lived within a small community of Japanese families who worked at a nearby lumber mill and railroad. However, his childhood classmates were mainly *haole*. "Most of the people were of Scandinavian descent— Norwegians, Danes, and they were great."

In Montana, George Oiye's parents also lived for a while near a railroad track in Helena. "My dad worked in what was called a 'round house' where they fixed engines ... He dumped the ashes out of the big locomotives. He used to take me down there, and oh, the smoke, all the sulfur. You got all choked up."

Whatever their geographical location, the *nisei* soldiers from Hawaii and the Mainland shared important bonds. They inherited a cultural legacy that emphasized education, honor and obligation. They experienced various degrees of racism from the larger society. They were the American-born sons of the *issei*, Japanese immigrants who endured much adversity for the benefit of their children.

Like millions of other immigrants before them, the *issei* left their homeland for various reasons. A few Japanese, such as shipwrecked sailors and fishermen, could be seen in America by the early 1800s, but large-scale purposeful immigration eastward to America and the kingdom of Hawaii was sparked in the late 1800s by the push and pull of hard economic times. Thousands of struggling subsistence farmers in Japan, hit by low harvests and high taxes, answered the call of Hawaii's sugar planters in the late 1800s. The planters needed people with strong backs who were able to labor from dawn to dusk under a blazing sun. Getting and keeping cheap labor had been a continual problem for Hawaii's sugar industry, whose management was dominated by *haoles*.

Native Hawaiians did not work the plantations in large numbers since their once-thriving population had dwindled drastically after contact with the West. Hawaiians were used to living within a mainly cooperative, nature-based society. Like native Americans, Hawaiians were devastated by the effects of a different value system which virtually annihilated their natural environment. Before long, much of Hawaii's natural resources were depleted through such activitites as whaling and hunting. Due largely to greed, rare wildlife and sandalwood forests were destroyed. Numerous Hawaiians, latched together like pack mules, died from the hardships of hauling sandalwood logs and working in the damp cold of the mountains. Like fish out of water, native Hawaiians perished from diverse causes, including psychological malaise and foreign diseases from which they had no immunity.

Before long, the sugar industry flourished with the labor of Asians, especially the Japanese. Of nearly 40,000 sugar workers in 1901, about 70% of the workers were Japanese.

While profits soared, the laborers were treated as commodities similar to pack mules. One sugar company, for instance, acknowledged a plantation manager's letter that requested bonemeal, canvas, "Japanese laborers," macaroni and a "Chinaman." Such dehumanization turned hope into bitterness for many a worker who toiled for only a few cents an hour.

Rising at dawn, the laborers faced 10 hours in the hot fields where endless rows of sugar cane awaited. Sharp leaves of the cane cut deeply into flesh. Swirls of red dust flew into eyes and nostrils and clung to hair moistened by sweat. Inside the humid, noisy mill, workers could taste the dust and perspiration which poured down their faces. At night, their exhausted bodies found a few hours of rest in tiny hovels.

When asked about the use of only non*haole* plantation labor, millionaire businessman

Walter Dillingham (1875-1963) said: "When you are asked to go in the sun and into the canebrake...you are subjecting the white man to do something that the good Lord did not create him to do. If He had, the people of the world, I think, would have had a white pigment of the skin and not variegated colors."

The striking image of the plantation *luna*, or overseer, is one that many an old-timer cannot forget: luna were usually *haole* or Portuguese men who carried a black "snake" whip as they rode on horseback through the fields. No wonder that a Japanese American soldier, on the Mainland for the first time during World War II, was surprised at what he saw. "Back home, the status of whites on the plantations was in the upper brackets—the managers or supervisors, never laborers," said George Mine, who belonged to the 442nd's artillery unit. "While training at Camp Shelby in Mississippi, we came upon a farm area and saw white farmers with overalls, dirty hands, dirty clothing, laboring on the farm. That made me a bit shocked. I had never seen a white man do that kind of thing, because I related to the situation back home."

When plantation workers turned to unions and strikes to improve their conditions during the early 1900s, they faced scorn and stereotyping. *Haole*-owned newspapers displayed cartoons of Japanese with buck teeth and slanted eyes—a forerunner of things to come. How, wondered many *haoles*, could such people be molded into an "American" and "Christian" image? The establishment attacked "Asiatic paganism," saying Buddhism was a major influence behind worker unrest, and blamed, among others, Japanese editors and language schools. Ironically, it was the language schools that emphasized such values as respect and loyalty.

Clearly, Hawaii's military and ruling oligarchy felt threatened by the sheer numbers of a physically and culturally different people. By 1920, there were some 256,000 people in Hawaii. About 109,000 of that number were Japanese.

The plantations made some improvements following strike actions during the early 1900s, but continued a paternalistic, condescending hierarchy. It was similar to the structure set by Hawaii's ruling oligarchy and ensured *haole* domination and control of the islands. Plantations were devised like pyramids—at the top, the manager's proverbial house on the hill; at the bottom, everyone else.

An image of this hierarchy may be seen in *All I Asking For Is My Body*, Milton Murayama's novel about 1930s plantation life: "Shit, too, was organized according to the plantation pyramid. It rained so continually, a damp smell of the outhouse hung over Pig Pen Avenue. The camp, I realized then, was planned ... around its sewage system ... Mr. Nelson was top shit on the highest slope, then there were the Portuguese, Spanish and *nisei lunas* with their indoor toilets which flushed into the same ditches, then Japanese camp, and Filipino camp ... Mr. Nelson acted like a father and he looked after you ... provided you didn't disobey."

Plantation paternalism took many forms. Ben Tamashiro, 100th Infantry Battalion, grew up on a Kauai plantation where his father operated a tailor shop. Like many others on the plantation, Tamashiro's family raised chickens. As a child, he found himself performing a yearly ritual during New Year's. He made holes in a gunnysack, placed two chickens inside, stuck their heads out of the holes and carried his cargo to the plantation manager's house. "My father made me take two of my best chickens every year like that and every year I'd say, 'Why do we have to do this?' And he'd say, *'Shikata ga nai'* ("It can't be helped.") For years I went through this, but one particular year sticks out. My father and I were at the manager's door and he saw the sack and knew what it was. He said, 'Just put 'em in the back.' So I went back and Christ! I saw a whole row of chickens from other plantation workers. So I'm thinking, 'What the hell are my two doing here?' And that got me mad. What the hell was he going to do with two more chickens? I remember that scene—the way he said, 'Take 'em to the back' and the dozens of chickens back there."

On Maui, Barney Hajiro toiled in the plantation fields to help support his family. "I made about a dollar a day or 10 cents an hour for 10 hours. If it rained, you didn't work and you didn't get paid. But it was hard getting other jobs if you were Oriental."

Tamashiro and Hajiro belonged to the *nisei* generation that took to heart the lessons of "justice" and "equality" learned in Hawaii public schools. Nearly 20,000 Japanese children were in public schools by 1920, rising to more than 41,000 by 1930.

McKinley High School, sometimes called "Tokyo High" by its detractors, was a place where many Asians were exposed to democratic ideals. Some progressive *haoles*, such as schoolteacher and principal Miles Cary, inspired the Asians to reach out. "Miles got his people to do what he wanted because he treated them humanely and considerately," said Major James Lovell, one of the leaders of the all-*nisei* 100th Infantry Battalion. "If there was any fault to find with him—and maybe it's not a fault—I thought of Miles as a dreamer. But I think it was due to his efforts to treat people right."

Not surprisingly, Cary was labeled "radical" by those who wished to maintain the status quo. Yet the status quo contradicted the ideals the *nisei* learned so well in the public schools: in the "real" world, *haoles*, mostly Republicans, mixed mainly with one another and excluded non*haoles* from promotions or positions of power. Non*haoles* who murdered *haoles* were given the death sentence, as in the 1929 hanging of mentally deranged Myles Fukunaga. But *haoles* who murdered non*haoles* were given minimal sentences or set free, as in the 1889 lynching of Katsu Goto. Goto's murderers mysteriously escaped jail and managed to flee the islands. However, the infamous Massie case of 1932 most clearly illustrated Hawaii's social mood before World War II.

Thalia Massie, wife of Navy Lieutenant Thomas Massie and daughter of Mainland socialite Grace Fortescue, accused five "Hawaiian boys," including two *nisei*, of raping her. Her case was weak, based on contradictory testimony. For one, the examining doctor smelled alcohol on Massie's breath but found no evidence of rape. In addition,

Early 1900s workers, probably along the Hamakua Coast of the
Big Island. Women did heavy work, from stripping cane leaves
to hauling heavy containers. Some gave birth in the fields.

the five defendants produced witnesses who proved they could not have been the
attackers. When the defendants were released on bail, Navy Admiral Yates Stirling
stated, "Our first inclination is to seize the brutes and string them up on trees."

One night, Lieutenant Massie, Fortescue and two Navy enlisted men kidnapped
defendant Joseph Kahahawai and shot him. Police caught the murderers with the body
before they could dump it into the ocean. Despite the efforts of noted (and expensive)
trial lawyer Clarence Darrow, the jury found the four guilty of manslaughter. When
Judge Charles Davis sentenced them to 10 years of hard labor, screams of protest from
afar reached the islands. Mainland newspapers branded the islands as "deplorable."
Hearst newspapers on the West Coast proclaimed Hawaii a place of "dangerous natives"
and unsafe for "white women." After much pressure from Hawaii's military and ruling
oligarchy to pardon the defendants, Governor Lawrence Judd commuted the sentence
from 10 years in prison to one hour in his office. Joe Kahahawai's convicted killers
sipped cocktails, chatted for the hour and left the islands.

The Massie case mirrored the larger society's perception of "darker stained races"

A prosperous Japanese family illustrates the blending of cultures. Some members appear at ease in the urbane attire of America's "flapper" era. Others wear traditional kimono and footwear.

as being inferior. The media in particular stereotyped minorities and glorified a single, superficial standard of beauty and behavior. Movies extolled the appeal of Betty Grable and the suave manner of Clark Gable. History books told of hardships faced by the Pilgrims and the new settlers, but ignored the enormous suffering of Native Americans and African Americans. The realities of ethnic minorities were a far cry from the sanitized images typified in Dick-and-Jane elementary schoolbooks. Such one-dimensional views of history exacted a sad price from minorities. Some rejected their parents' traditions. Others could not relate to their history books. "When I was growing up, schoolteachers told us, 'Forget your Japanese heritage—be American,'" said Walter Inouye, whose *issei* father spoke fluent Hawaiian. "In 1922, songs were very patriotic, remembering World War I, songs like 'When Johnny Comes Marching Home.' During my growing up, (society) stressed this kind of thinking. But the history we learned had no bearing on my life—Pilgrims and stuff like that … European history was difficult to comprehend."

Public and personal rejection of ethnic heritage was particularly evident on the

Mainland where Japanese were few in number. "I tried to get rid of my Japanese identity," explained George Oiye of his Montana childhood. "For example, I loved the food but wouldn't eat it … because I didn't want to be identified with being Japanese. And (at the time) I wasn't proud of my parents. A lot of times I didn't want to be with my brothers and sisters when they showed up because that made more of us (in a group)."

But no matter how the *nisei* tried to be "American" in Hawaii or the Mainland, no matter how high their test scores, no matter how hard they worked, Asians, like African Americans, could never escape the visibility factor. "Injustice in that era was just one of the facts of life," said Robert Sasaki. "One thing I clearly remember is that we couldn't get jobs at Hawaiian Electric Company or at Pearl Harbor. Only in rare cases you would find Japanese working at Pearl Harbor."

In Hawaii, at least, the *nisei* found comfort in their large numbers and in kinships forged from childhood. At home, they enjoyed traditional Asian fare of rice, fish and vegetable dishes. Outside, they thrived in the richness of other cultures—Polynesian, Filipino, Chinese, Korean, Portuguese, Puerto Rican and others. They danced to Glenn Miller songs and knew the words to "I'll Be Seeing You." They were exposed to *poi*, hot dogs, the warm, easygoing attitudes of Polynesians and the sunshine that encouraged physical activity.

Island *nisei* excelled in sports—boxing, judo, swimming, baseball, football. Years of outdoor exposure, including labor on farms and plantations, toughened their bodies and enhanced their overall strength. Despite their smaller physique, the *nisei* often beat much larger opponents, a skill that was to prove useful during basic training on the Mainland. Whatever the sport, many of them became champions in their fields. "My friend Hirose told me of the time he went to Europe with an all-American swimming team when he was 14," said Tadao Beppu. "During basic training in Mississippi in 1943, he had some guard duty in Alabama. Hirose came across a German prisoner who told him, 'Hey, I saw you swim.'"

Another key element that bonded different cultures in Hawaii was the ability to communicate with each other through pidgin English. This facility with language later proved useful when the soldiers were in Europe. "Our boys picked up German, French and Italian quickly and they were good," observed Beppu.

Their general flexibility and openness to different cultures have been credited as major factors in the *nisei* soldiers' outstanding prowess in battle. "With the pidgin English, the Japanese understood other cultures, including the *haole* culture," said Doctor Herbert Wong, a Honolulu physician who experienced racism as an intern and resident on the Mainland in the 1950s. "But *haoles* couldn't or wouldn't understand them."

By 1937, there were nearly 400,000 people living in Hawaii. Of that number, more than 150,000 were of Japanese ancestry.

UNLIKE HAWAII, GROWING UP Asian on the mainland was an isolating experience. Their ethnic visibility and extremely small numbers often elicited stone-throwing, cold stares or such slurs as "Goddam Jap." Not surprisingly, the Japanese banded together whenever possible and started small businesses or farms of their own.

During the 1920s, the era when most of the Japanese American soldiers were born, about 111,000 Japanese were dispersed throughout the continental United States. The majority lived on the West Coast, especially California.

Susumu Ito, today a professor emeritus at Harvard Medical School, recalled his grammar school near Stockton. Only one teacher was available for the mainly Japanese student body. "When you have 21 students to teach, from first through eighth grade, that's hard. Then when we lived closer to town I went to a new school and almost flunked out. I didn't know what was going on. My mother, with her broken and limited English, bribed the teacher with silk stockings, saying, 'My boy should pass.' And she did pass me … My mother was very perceptive about my future in a white man's world. She thought the ultimate was that someday I'd own a service station. When I got out of mechanic's school I couldn't work anywhere except at a Japanese-owned garage because I couldn't get into the union."

Joseph Hattori, whose father started a *tofu* company in Los Angeles, was also aware of racism while growing up. "Oh sure, you're reminded of being Japanese. You go to the theaters, you don't get to sit in the middle. You sit on the sides. That's how it was. There was discrimination that was subtle. You became aware of it."

If Hattori, Ito and thousands of other Japanese were a distinct minority in California's vastness, then George Oiye was the proverbial "needle in a haystack" in Montana. Oiye's mother was pregnant with George in 1921, when she and her husband traveled by horse and wagon to a mining camp in Montana.

Only about 500 Japanese lived within the wide, open ranges of Montana's 150,000 square miles, said Oiye. "I was born in 1922 in a log cabin, roughly 14,000 feet up in the Rocky Mountains and it was 40 degrees below zero. My family stayed in this log cabin all winter and my father was the midwife. They had 50 cents in their pocket. They were seven miles from the nearest store or other people. Consider yourself being born in a snowdrift, and the only transportation is by horse or foot."

The journey of Oiye's family was an unusual one in the Japanese immigration experience, but, like the others, it was filled with hope. Tom, George's father, came to America in 1915 as a boy of 16 and worked at odd jobs, including a brief stint on a whaling ship in Alaska. When he earned enough money, Tom returned to Japan and brought back Taka, his picture bride. "This is what amazes me—my parents didn't know each other, but two weeks later they come across to America—steerage, because that's the only way Asians came over, steerage. They were sick all the way because the ocean was so rough."

Oiye's parents settled in Seattle, working at various jobs. Taka went to work for a well-to-do Swedish woman. "And that was a very significant thing in her life because the Swedish lady was very, very elegant. She taught my mother to speak and write English that was just perfect."

The Oiyes went into the hotel business for a while, charging 25 cents a night. "They were called flophouses in those days. In most of them, the beds may or may not have clean sheets or bedbugs, but my mother was impeccably clean and their place was spotless. For 25 cents, her guests got a clean bed."

The family might have flourished there, especially with the good service rendered by the Oiyes, but a "Mr. Breen" walked into their lives one day and changed everything. He was trying to raise money to salvage a bankrupt mine in Montana. "When you're in a strange country and you're trying to make a go, you take a lot of chances, so my parents sold their hotel and invested in this mine."

The Oiyes loaded their belongings, placed them on a train and headed for Montana in the hopes of "going for the big one." It turned out be a bust. By 1924, the family was in Helena, the capital, where Oiye's father worked for the railroad, like most of the other Japanese in Montana. "The workers lived in tar paper shacks right along the railroad tracks, usually by the round house. They built their own bathhouse, the *furo*. So it was very basic, very much Japanese."

When Oiye was about five, the family moved to the tiny town of Trident where the four children attended school at Trident and Three Forks. (The head waters of the Missouri River come together at Trident and Three Forks.) Oiye played with the other children until, in their innocence, his playmates tried to take him home. "They got rejected for taking me home. So pretty soon we learned we were different. I guess one of the things that bothers me most is rejection … I could deal more with people shooting me, cutting me up and what not. But to be rejected is one of the worst things there is,

Many Japanese families on the Mainland went into business and became farmers, shopkeepers, barbers and the like. Here, fishermen pose with their catch of the day.

as far as I'm concerned. I loved Japanese food, but wouldn't eat it."

Rejection from the larger culture resulted in Oiye's rejection of his own ethnicity. Oiye's parents tried to teach their children the Japanese language, but they refused. "We didn't want it, we didn't want to be Japanese." Oiye nevertheless reached out to other Japanese in his community, revealing the complex situations faced by minorities who struggle to adapt to the majority society which scorns them. "When I saw another Japanese person, I made sure I got to know them. I made a lot of good Japanese friends, but they didn't become my very very best friends because that would bring more rejection of me if I were identified with them. In private, in my house, we'd be best friends, have great fun and love each other. But in school I wouldn't sit with those guys because it would bring more rejection (from *haoles*)."

As in the case of the Oiyes, a *haole* stranger met Chester Tanaka's parents in 1914, and changed the family's lives. The prominent lawyer asked the San Francisco couple to be his family's maid and butler. "But my parents didn't know the attorney lived in St. Louis, Missouri, so he paid their transportation from San Francisco," recalled Tanaka.

"They worked for the attorney for about a year. He was very supportive when my parents wanted to go out on their own."

Although Tanaka grew up in an area where other Japanese were rare in number, he remembered a happy childhood. "I grew up mainly around *haoles* and they treated me nicely. I played street hockey with them and was even a group leader. I remember this lady, Ruby, who made the best bathtub gin in St. Louis during Prohibition."

Tanaka's parents owned a tiny restaurant in a black neighborhood. They were robbed three times during the first year of business, said Tanaka. "But the blacks soon learned that my parents were honest people. At that time, some restaurants were pulling shenanigans like serving rabbit and saying 'It's chicken.' Most people were ripping the blacks off. But my parents served the neighborhood well and the blacks protected them. If customers asked for meat frankfurters, they got meat, not one filled with corn meal. For nearly 30 years, my parents were safe."

Like George Oiye, George Ernest Goto, from Colorado, understood the pain of rejection. He was one of five children born to a Japanese father and *haole* mother. Goto's father, George Hirose, was born in Japan and moved to the United States at the age of 17. After working on a Montana railroad, George Hirose moved to Missouri and met the woman he wanted to marry, but because of the state's anti-miscegenation laws, they married in Sydney, Nebraska.

Goto remembered his father as a man who worked so hard he hardly had time to spend with his children. "My mother took us around all the time. We looked odd, with her walking and leading around two Asian-faced boys at the time. Sometimes people called my little brother and me names, like 'chinky chinky Chinaman,' that kind of stuff."

Goto attended high school in Denver and was one of very few Asians among a large group of Spanish, black and *haole* children. Although he experienced discrimination, Goto recalled the particularly vicious way racism was inflicted on blacks. "In the late 1930s and early 1940s, they couldn't go into the swimming pools until Friday—that was their day. The pool was then drained and filled up again. Blacks had to sit in the top seven rows in the balcony in the movie theaters. If you had a restaurant like my father did, you had to have a table with chairs set up in the kitchen for any blacks who wanted to come in and eat. They couldn't sit in the dining room and eat. My father didn't like doing this, but had no choice. Every restaurant had to have a place in the kitchen for the blacks. They couldn't be in the dining room. We found this practice distasteful. I went to school with blacks, and we were friends. Practically every black in Denver in the mid-1930s went to Manuel High School."

Sadly, such images would become common for young Goto. As the 1930s came to a close, no one could have predicted the ironic manner in which he and thousands of other Japanese Americans would meet and witness a similar theme of racism carried out to its extreme—in America and in Europe.

Shock Waves

At first, I thought it was strange because I used to see smoke at maneuvers and it was white. This one was kind of black. I said, "Hey, this is different."

Tadao Beppu
442nd Regimental Combat Team

FEVERISH MILITARY ACTIVITY dominated the island scene in 1940. U.S. President Franklin Roosevelt had just declared an embargo on most goods to Japan, illuminating the tension between the two countries. That same year, the U.S. Congress passed the National Draft Act. It affected Hawaii's estimated population of 421,000, which included 157,000 people of Japanese ancestry. Ben Tamashiro, fresh out of Kauai High School, was one of them.

"All the guys had a selective service number, and many people could see a war coming in one form or another," he said. "I said to myself, 'Oh hell, might as well get it over with,' and volunteered for the first draft—December 10, 1940."

Tamashiro received basic training at "boom town," the U.S. Army's Schofield Barracks on Oahu, where the *nisei* acquired a reputation of being the "best recruits." Upon completion, he was assigned to the Hawaii National Guard's 299th Infantry Regiment and returned to Kauai to guard a little airfield called Burns Field. (The 299th consisted of Neighbor Island men; Oahu men belonged to the Guard's 298th Infantry Regiment. The regiments were federalized and mobilized into active duty by summer 1940.)

Most of the Japanese Americans became a part of the 298th or 299th upon the completion of basic training, but not all. Some, like Albert Oki and Kenneth Otagaki, were assigned to the 65th Combat Engineers (previously known as 3rd Engineers), a mainly *haole* outfit. Oki was in his third year at the University of Hawaii when he was drafted in March 1941. Otagaki, a UH wrestling champion, had just earned a bachelor's degree in technical agriculture. How did they become part of the 65th? "Good question," said Oki. "I noticed that the recruits drafted into engineering were mostly athletes. Second, many had college backgrounds."

They were also given a series of tests and scored high on subjects related to math and science. "But if you tried to get into other branches of service, say, the Air Corps, you had no chance," said Otagaki, an agricultural worker who could have taken advantage of his exemption from military service.

Of the 3,000 men inducted through selective service boards in Hawaii, about half were of Japanese ancestry. Tamashiro and Otagaki were two of 900 Japanese American inductees who had volunteered within the 12 months prior to the attack on Pearl Harbor.

Like Oki, Yuzuru Morita was drafted in March 1941. In the months before Pearl Harbor, he worked at Fort Armstrong, loading and unloading military equipment. "Then we transferred them from Honolulu Harbor to all the depots," said Morita. "I was in charge of rail shipments to the different depots. We were working 12-hour shifts, day and night."

From his home in Honolulu's McCully district, Tadao Beppu noticed that the familiar young Asian faces he used to see attending the nearby University of Hawaii were no more. "I knew they finished the university here. I asked, 'Hey what happened to those guys.' The answer was, 'Oh, they went to Japan to go to graduate school.' But they weren't in graduate school. They were in the Philippines doing intelligence work for the U.S. government. They mingled among the Japanese businessmen in Manila, trying to get a feel for what was going on ..."

That is exactly what Arthur Komori and other Japanese Americans were doing—espionage work for the U.S. Army's Corps of Intelligence Police. "All of a sudden I disappeared and my friends wondered where I went," said Komori, who graduated from the University of Hawaii in spring 1940. "Nobody knew what happened to me."

Komori, working with General Douglas MacArthur's staff, had left Hawaii on April 7, 1941, disguised as a civilian "workaway" on the transport ship, *Republic*. "I went with 2,000 troops or so, most of whom ended up in the Bataan Death March. In Manila, I gathered information on the (upcoming) Japanese invasion of the Philippines ... I lived among the Japanese population, staying in a Japanese-owned hotel. They thought I was an American draft dodger, so the Japanese allowed me to help them translate and interpret. The Americans controlled the Philippines in those days."

Komori's extraordinary adventure began in early 1941, when he was scheduled to be drafted like many other young men. But the Army, desperately needing Japanese language translators, interpreters and interrogators to work in the field, instead enlisted the *nisei* for its intelligence network. "This *haole* officer, Major Raymond, knew the *nisei* in Hawaii to be very loyal and he wanted them to join his headquarters in Manila," said Komori. "Within a couple of weeks, I was on a boat."

Komori worked secretly in the Philippines, getting to know the Japanese community—the people with the Japan Culture and Tourist Bureau, the Japanese Embassy and a Japanese news agency. Unknown to him, Japanese airplanes were nearing Pearl Harbor, Oahu, on the morning of December 7, 1941.

That morning, Beppu and his friends were in McCully, waiting for a car ride to a countryside baseball field. The youths were looking forward to the day, when they saw

Pearl Harbor aftermath, as seen from Aiea.

the smoke overhead. "At first, I thought it was strange because I used to see the smoke at maneuvers and it was white," said Beppu. "This one was kind of black. I said, 'Hey, this is different.' Then a corner neighborhood store in McCully burned to the ground, hit by an anti-aircraft shell."

A few miles away in Aiea, a neighborhood that overlooks Pearl Harbor, Royce Higa awoke to the sounds of "rap, rap, rap" on the tin roof of his family's plantation home. "Anti-aircraft shells," he said. "Then, we looked outside and we could see the stores around were dirty, all around dirty. We saw the airplanes with the *Hi No Maru*, the symbol of the rising sun. So we knew they were Japanese."

Harold Ueoka was in the same area, watching the attack from a roadside. "But we didn't realize this was war," he said. "About 9 a.m., the Hawaii National Guard came up and said, 'This is the real thing, go up to the mountain.'"

Higa remembered the evacuation to the top of Aiea Heights, the gathering place for the mainly Japanese population who lived just outside of Pearl Harbor. "We stayed in the woods for maybe two days," he said.

Morita, on alert since November 1941, had been one of the 10 percent of his battalion allowed to spend that December 7 weekend at his Waipahu home. Like the others, he thought the smoke in the sky was a practice session. "Then the firing got more intense. My brother and I got on the roof and, ho-o-o-o, we saw all the anti-aircraft shells bursting in the air. I turned on the radio and that's when I heard, 'All military personnel, report back to your station.'"

Meanwhile, Tamashiro, a company clerk on Kauai with the National Guard, was clearing his desk. "As December approached, I prepared discharge papers for all of those who were in the first draft. When December 7 came, I took the batch of papers and slung them in the wastebasket. I remember that."

News and rumors spread quickly across oceans. Shortly after the bombing, Arthur Komori was thrown into a Filipino prison. "It was already December 8 in the Philippines, and a Filipino constabulary arrested me and other Japanese at the point of a bayonet ... The prison was a scary hell hole, very primitive."

As he and other Japanese Americans in the intelligence corps faced complicated dangers, speculation about Komori was spreading thousands of miles away. It was known he was a pilot who had obtained his flying license during his student days at the University of Hawaii. "Rumors were going around that I had crashed a plane on December 7 at Pearl Harbor. They thought I was the enemy (pilot) since word was that a McKinley High School jacket was found in the crash, and it must have belonged to a *nisei*."

The world was stunned by the destruction at Pearl Harbor: six ships were sunk and numerous others were severely damaged at the most important naval base in the Pacific. Worse, about 2,400 people were killed, according to an official at the National Park Service, the U.S.S. Arizona Memorial.

Even the civilian sector did not escape the destruction. People were hurt or killed by wayward American anti-aircraft shells. At one corner of town, a young Red Cross instructor saw a demolished house, entered it and found a woman nearly buried by rubble and decapitated by shrapnel. "Another, who had fallen dead at the congested corner of King and McCully, still clutched the stumps where her legs had been," recalled U.S. Senator Daniel K. Inouye in his 1967 book, *Journey to Washington.*

Volunteer fireman Edward Tarutani was nursing a hangover that day, the consequence of drinking with friends the night before. "Oh, my God, my head was big that Sunday morning when my brother, a volunteer for the ambulance service, called," said Tarutani. "He told me it was the 'real thing,' and that he had just returned from Judd Street where he helped three or four passengers in a car which was smashed by a shell. One of them had an amputated leg."

Alan Beekman, a Hawaii writer, shared an experience of his late wife, Takeko Okawa. "She was a Japanese language instructor and teaching when the shell exploded. She said it ripped off the arm of a child. There's a memorial there at Nuuanu and Vineyard streets."

Japanese Americans volunteered their services into the night. Thousands of them belonged to the Hawaii Territorial Guard, composed mainly of students from the University of Hawaii ROTC program. "We were assigned to guard key installations, the water storage plants and other important utilities," said Don Shimazu. "I was stationed in front of the main library that night."

Albert Oki and Kenneth Otagaki of the 65th Combat Engineers were also on guard duty that night. Today, they are decorated 100th veterans who were wounded in action. Back then, both men were on leave. "We were American soldiers so we returned to Schofield right away," said Otagaki. "We were naive about the race part, and didn't even think about that."

He and Oki were assigned to guard a truck on the evening of December 7. "It was dark and raining hard, so Ken and I got out of the rain and into the truck," said Oki. "Apparently, we didn't realize they were looking upon us with suspicion. Saboteurs. They called out, 'Hey Oki, Otagaki, where are you?' So we jumped out of the truck and they practically pushed us. A sergeant aimed his .45 at us, and they marched us into this blacked-out office, searched us separately and took our guns away."

The changed attitude of their one-time *haole* friends in their outfit stunned the young soldiers. "In my case, they stripped me naked," said Otagaki. "They thought I might have documents on me. I was so furious, so disillusioned, that I started crying. I remember saying, 'Please get me out as soon as you can, because I'm no good to this company.'"

Worse was the sense of betrayal. "We drank together, bunked together, but all of a sudden we became enemies after December 7," said Otagaki. "That really hurt and disappointed me. The more disturbing part was the fact that we had some local *haole* officers who went along with this kind of thing. And I said, 'How can this be? You know who we are.'"

Wartime suspicion took on deadlier tones. The next day, December 8, the Coast Guard towed two fishing boats into Honolulu's Kewalo Basin. Inside, eight men lay dead or wounded.

A few days before December 7, the eight fishermen (four in each boat) had left Oahu on the two sampans to catch fish for the upcoming holidays. Isolated from outside communication, the crew of at least one sampan, the *Kiho Maru*, learned of the bombing from a nearby sampan equipped with a radio. While people on Oahu were still reeling from the attack, the fishermen headed toward Honolulu's Kewalo Basin the next morning with their fish, unaware of the extreme danger that awaited in the sky. Kaichi Okada and his three helpers were in one of the boats. Okada was the uncle of Harold Yokoyama.

"An American airplane shot dead (six) men in the two fishing boats," said Yokoyama, whose family's livelihood depended on fishing. "They were shot by .50-caliber bullets from the airplane. The other boat belonged to the Kida family. The Coast Guard towed the boats (later) to Kewalo Basin in the early evening, and we saw the bodies. The boat had so much damage, it sank one week later. I went to my uncle's funeral. He was a single man, an American citizen …"

Three people were also killed on the other sampan, the *Kiho Maru*—Sutematsu Kida, 54, his son, Kiichi Kida, 24, and their friend and helper, Kiho Uehara, 29. The fourth, Seiki Arakaki, lived to tell his story to a *Honolulu Star-Bulletin* reporter on December 7, 1977. "There were four or five Army P-40s flying over us," said Uehara, who was shot in the knee. "Each picked out a target and attacked." (Four sampans were strafed, but the fishermen on the other two managed to escape serious injury.)

Kida's daughter, Kimie Shidaki, went to Queen's Hospital to identify the bodies of her father and brother. "The *haole* MP there said, 'What the hell you Japs doing here?' I said, 'I'm the fisherman's daughter.' Inside, I saw the bodies lined up—I can never forget—dressed in shorts. My father had a black spot on his throat, his hands in an open position. My brother had a bullet through his chest. In my family there were six girls and one boy, Kiichi. He had just bought the boat in July and was so happy. At the time I identified the bodies, I had no tears. My feet were numb, but I kept moving. At the mortuary I told my mom, 'Be strong now.' My mom said, 'No, this cannot be.' My mom was frozen for several minutes. Then the tears came. I held it inside for a long time … The past is not the past. The past is always with us."

Fear enveloped the islands as Hawaii's Governor Joseph B. Poindexter placed the territory under martial law on December 7 and suspended the writ of *habeas corpus,* a citizen's right to due process under the law and protection from illegal imprisonment. In essence, an individual's rights meant nothing under military rule.

Lieutenant General Walter Short simultaneously proclaimed himself "military governor," installed a military government and suppressed civil courts in the territory. (After 11 days in office, Short was replaced by General Delos C. Emmons.) Military rule meant that even the smallest misdemeanor, say, a traffic violation, was tried in provost courts and presided over by Army officers who doled out stiff fines and other punishments without regard to federal or local statutes. It was a three-year rule that brought in millions for the military and wrought havoc on the U.S. Constitution. Before 1941, precedence of military rule on U.S. soil could be found only in conquered territories such as occurred during the Civil and Indian wars. (J. Garner Anthony, Hawaii's attorney general from 1942-43, gives a detailed account in his book, *Hawaii Under Army Rule: The Real Story of Three Years of Martial Law in a Loyal American Territory.*)

In the ensuing days and weeks, Oahu resembled an armed camp, guarded by machine guns, barbed wires, sandbags, blackouts and trenches. Gas masks and strict curfews became as common as the rumors and suspicions which pervaded an anxious population. Civilians were subjected to numerous restrictions under military rule, but people of Japanese ancestry were particularly targeted. Their fishing fleets were impounded and, for practical purposes, lost forever. The general public was asked to report any meetings of Japanese, especially Buddhist gatherings. Japanese were prohibited from travel or changing residences. They could not enter certain security areas. The restriction included Japanese Americans rendering valuable service for the U.S. Army's Military Intelligence Service. And on and on.

"They chased a lot of Japanese Americans from Pearl Harbor with bayonets," recalled Ted Tsukiyama.

Hideo Nakamine underlined that observation with an incident that affected his own family. "Shortly after December 7, my older brother James, a city bus driver, drove into the Pearl Harbor compound and unloaded some passengers. A Marine sentry pointed his fixed bayonet at my brother when he got off the bus to pay a traffic fine. The guard followed James until he got in the bus and drove away."

Stan Akita, living on the Big Island at the time, remembered his two uncles who were working as stevedores. "They were let go. The company didn't want so-called Japs to be working there. I think I was a little too young to realize what was happening. Within your own community, your own hometown, you're called Jap. You go to the theaters and you hear, 'Sit down, Jap.'"

The elderly Japanese were especially puzzled. "My parents came home one night—they didn't know English well—and asked us, 'What means Jap?'" said Yuki Akita, Stan's wife. "I guess with the radio and newspapers, everything was 'Jap, Jap, Jap.' The local newspapers wrote about the enemy 'Japs.' But we in Hawaii were also of Japanese ancestry."

Fears of sabotage persisted in spite of findings by the FBI to the contrary. "We even had to boil our water because (government officials) thought saboteurs would poison our water," said Hideo Nakamine.

As early as January 1942, the *Honolulu Advertiser* declared, "No espionage can be traced to the local population." Ironically, public hysteria over spying was misdirected. From 1942-44, 18 Caucasians were charged with spying for Japan. At least ten were convicted.

Whatever suspicions the military harbored against the Japanese, it recognized their sheer strength in the work force. The *Honolulu Star-Bulletin* announced in March 1943: "Hawaii Labor—Citizens Dependent on Japanese Laborers." For years, Japanese workers had provided the labor not only on plantations but also for construction projects and defense-related work. After December 7, 1941, the Japanese were a virtually indispensable labor force for the military.

The men of the 370th Engineer Battalion, for instance, dug trenches, cut trees, built airstrips, hauled rubbish, cleared large fields and constructed roads, barracks, water tanks, and training schools for jungle warfare in the Pacific. (The 370th later formed the core of the 1399th Engineer Construction Battalion.) Among them was Barney Hajiro, who was to become one of the many unheralded soldiers of World War II. "I didn't have rifle training, so we did all kinds of dirty work—putting up barbed wire, handling acid, painting and so on," he said.

The 1399th also included Harold Yokoyama. As he worked under the hot sun, Yokoyama could not forget the sight of his uncle and the other fishermen, their bodies and boats riddled with bullets from American guns.

IN SPITE OF SIGNIFICANT Japanese American contributions to the war effort, a few *haole* businessmen urged the removal of all Japanese to camps on the Mainland. Mass internment, however, was not practical or economically feasible. On December 19, 1941, General Delos Emmons, commander of the Army, rejected a suggestion by the Joint Chiefs of Staff in faraway Washington to intern all of Hawaii's Japanese. Emmons bucked heads with Washington again on February 9, 1942, when he refused a War Department order directing him to fire all Japanese American civilians employed by the Army in Hawaii.

Economics played a major role in Hawaii's reluctance to incarcerate Japanese by the thousands, but the total picture may be more complex than meets the eye. For one thing, island Japanese emerged from a multi-racial and cosmopolitan environment that exhibited an acceptance of different cultures, when compared to other places. For another, there is an esoteric facet that defies Western logic but cannot be dismissed simply as "myth": Hawaii's powerful spiritual past. Early Hawaiians had initially welcomed all people, all beliefs. Said Doctor Edward Kealanahele, Hawaiian historian and healing *kahuna*, "Consider the Hawaiian spirit. After Pearl Harbor, other groups could

The black badge: requirement for many Japanese American workers.

have been extremely cruel to the Japanese, like the black and white situation that existed on the Mainland in which there was no love, no feeling...But we have this feeling, this cultural bond. We have love between us and the Japanese because we grew up that way." (Kealanahele has been designated a "Living Treasure of Hawaii" by the Honpa Hongwanji Mission of Hawaii.)

Others did not harbor this feeling. In the tense, pragmatic world that existed after Pearl Harbor was attacked, there were other ways to control workers—the black badge, for instance, issued under the auspices of the U.S. Engineering Department (USED). Bordered in black, the circular plastic pin bore the word, "Restricted."

Civilians of Japanese ancestry who worked at defense-related jobs, say, at waterfronts or construction projects at military bases, were required to wear the black "restricted" badges. "We felt like how the Jews must have felt in Germany," said Tadao Beppu, who was to become a noted political figure in postwar Hawaii. "Private or public workers who had Japanese blood—one fourth, one eighth, whatever—were required to wear them. So there's a bunch of us working and I'm the only one wearing the black badge."

Lizo Honma remembered the black badge and the humiliating times of being accompanied by an MP (military police) wherever he went. "I was working on a project at Schofield Barracks and I said, 'I'm going to the toilet.' The MP walked behind me with his rifle ... because I was Japanese."

Like many other Japanese workers, Royce Higa had been loading and unloading cargo on ships before December 7. After the outbreak of war, the men were pulled from the ship gangs. "For several months we were in the countryside, cutting *kiawe* trees and clearing the land," recalled Higa. "A few months later, we were back at the docks, this time wearing a black badge."

Virtually everyone was required to have some form of identification during wartime, but only the Japanese had to wear the distinctive badge with the black border, said Walter Inouye. "I was at Ala Moana Park, repairing military equipment for the 64th Coast Artillery Battalion. They put armed guards over me. When they asked me to repair items at Haleiwa—the area contained a flying field, tent cities, among other things—I said, 'Forget it.' The black badge was something I hated. I got rid of it as soon as I could."

Black badges and other identifications were issued by the Central Intelligence Bureau (CIB), said Alan Beekman, who was employed by the agency in 1942. "Everyone had to get an identification badge, fill out a personal history form and get fingerprinted and photographed."

Race, not character, determined the ranking of badges. "Number One" badges, for instance, went to Caucasians with no serious criminal record, said Beekman. "The 'Number Two' went to Caucasians with criminal records, but it looked like everyone else's. I remember a man who had two murder convictions. He got a number two badge.

Those of Japanese ancestry, with a clean record and of American or dual citizenship, got the 'Number Three' or restrictive black badges. Caucasians married to Japanese got the unrestricted badges, but their children still had to wear the restricted badges … You got 'Number Four' if you were *kibei*, born here but educated in Japan. In fact, *kibei* often could not get a badge to work on any government-related project. Number four also included Koreans and some were outraged by that. See, Korea was dominated by Japan. One Korean man was angry. He said, 'I'm Korean, not Japanese.'"

Though a demeaning form of control, the required wearing of black badges was not as severe a consequence as the forced removal of island Japanese from their livelihood, their families, their pets and everything else they held dear.

While Hawaii's Japanese were not removed en masse, many were interned at Oahu's Sand Island and, later, Honouliuli. The Sand Island camp consisted of four compounds—two of 250 capacity for male Japanese, one for 40 females of mixed races and one for 25 Germans and Italians. "My father was at Sand Island, but he was sent home because he was so sick," said Lizo Honma. "Otherwise, they would have sent him to the camp in Arkansas. My father was active in Japanese language school. They took him to Sand Island while I was at basic training."

Nearly 2,000 Japanese, including community leaders, *kibei*, schoolteachers and Buddhist and Shinto priests were sent to Mainland camps. "My dad was a Buddhist minister and considered a 'potentially dangerous alien'—that was the term they used in those days," said the Reverend Yoshiaki Fujitani, who served with the U.S. Army's Military Intelligence Service (MIS) during World War II. "He was interned at Santa Fe, New Mexico."

Reverend Fujitani's father could have been one of the many Japanese who were loaded onto a ship late one night as dockworker Royce Higa watched from a distance. "I saw older folks boarding the ship, walking up the gangplank. These were ministers, schoolteachers and recent Japanese arrivals. In the evening, after we unloaded the ship, they'd board. I remember many people boarded that ship. (The authorities) wouldn't let us get near. It was so late at night, they were probably hiding the fact that some Japanese were being interned. This is my opinion."

THE 127,000 JAPANESE living on the Mainland in 1942 generally felt the consequences of racism in a far more oppressive way. They had been subjected to various physical and psychological attacks by *haoles* long before the outbreak of war.

The attacks were particularly virulent in California, where 90% of Mainland Japanese lived. Congregations of them worked in shantytowns, agricultural communities, small businesses and some government jobs. Their growing ethnic numbers and successes, however, agitated the larger society and sparked open hostility. Slurs such as "Chinky chinky Chinaman" accompanied graffiti and signs in town which proclaimed, "Japs

An American-born child, tagged for incarceration. Los Angeles, California, April 1942.

Not Wanted." Periodic exclusionary laws turned words into action. In 1924, for instance, Congress passed the Asian Exclusion Act, which prohibited further immigration from Japan. In an ironic twist, Congress passed that same year the American Indian Citizenship Act so that Native Americans could now become citizens in their homeland.

World War II turned an uneasy situation into a nightmare for the Mainland Japanese as Hearst newspapers on the West Coast fanned the outcry against the "Yellow Peril."

Unlike his Hawaii counterpart, Lieutenant General John L. DeWitt, head of the Western Defense Command, was bent on mass internment in spite of intelligence reports that cleared the Japanese of any internal threat. DeWitt claimed internment was a "military necessity."

On February 19, 1942, President Franklin D. Roosevelt signed Executive Order No. 9066, which set the stage for internment. In March 1942, DeWitt issued the first of 108 military proclamations which resulted in the detention of more than 110,000 Japanese from the West Coast. This number included nearly 2,000 from Hawaii and 2,300 from Latin America (mostly from Peru). The dehumanizing experience meant the loss of homes, jobs, beloved pets, and profitable farms, some of which were coveted by *haole* farmers. With a few belongings in their hands, the uprooted Japanese faced an existence of tar paper shacks, barbed wires, armed guards and food covered with dust and sand. This loss of dignity struck the Mainland Japanese in public and personal ways.

Tom Kawano, who was inducted into the Army in August 1941, was in San Francisco on December 7, eating at an upstairs Chinese restaurant. "Below us, we witnessed older Japanese men, the *issei*, being picked up. I feel the War Department must have known. It already had a list made out. All over the West Coast, they knew who to pick up."

In Los Angeles, an *issei* veteran of World War I went to a hotel, paid for his room and committed suicide. In death, his hands clutched his certificate of honorary American citizenship. In another part of Los Angeles, Joseph Hattori, only 17, had no idea what awaited him as he watched a matinee movie in a theater on December 7. "Suddenly the lights came on. They announced that Japanese planes had bombed Pearl Harbor and that all military personnel must get back to their bases right away. I didn't know what to think. Being raised and educated in the U.S., I was disappointed. Beyond that, I was stunned.

Manzanar Concentration Camp in California where intense summer heat and dust storms made life even more miserable for its inmates.

I felt powerless. Everything was beyond my control. (People in the theater) looked at me and they didn't say anything but I knew what they were thinking."

Hattori found support the next day among his racially mixed classmates and a Latin teacher who expressed her sadness. "She was a white teacher and she was really sorry for us since there were a number of Japanese in school. When we first went to a temporary camp in Pomona, my classmates visited us."

"Camp" for the Hattoris was the Pomona Racetrack, typical of the 15 fairgrounds or racetracks used as temporary "assembly centers" on the West Coast and in Arizona. They were filthy and smelly. "We slept in the horse stalls and ate in mess halls. After several months, we went to Heart Mountain, Wyoming."

Heart Mountain was one of 10 "permanent" concentration camps spread througout the continental United States and typically located in a desolate area. ("No trees in the whole area," said Hattori.) The camp, typical of the others, consisted of barbed wires, guards with machine guns, barracks covered with tar paper, unsanitary conditions and little privacy. The psychological desolation was worse. Feelings of powerlessness and despair set in, resulting in several suicides among the camps.

Heart Mountain was especially brutal in the winter for its 14,000 internees. Temperatures plunged as low as 30 degrees below zero. "Winter was so cold, bitter cold," said Hattori. "We had coal burning stoves. You had to go outside for the bathroom. You had to be very careful since you could get frostbite and lose your nose, ears, whatever."

George Ishihara and his family ended up in the cold of a camp at Minidoka, Idaho. Ishihara, working in California when the war started, returned to his home state of Washington when his family received evacuation orders. "Our parents weren't exactly young and we wanted to be evacuated together. So we were moved to the King County Fairground in Puyallup for about six months. We were in bunkhouses, where only a thin wall with an open top separated my family's space from the others. You could hear everything going on next door. My two sisters, mother, father and I lived in one room. We didn't have much room so the only community thing we did maybe once a week was to move the tables back in the dining mess hall and have a dance or something."

At Minidoka, Idaho, Ishihara blended into the mass of some 13,000 other Japanese interned at the camp. That number included Shiro Kashino.

A native of Washington, Kashino was interned with his brothers and sisters in Idaho. (Kashino lost his parents when he was in grammar school.) "Later I went to Montana to harvest the sugar beets since that was better than staying in the camps. I guess there was a manpower shortage because of the war, so these farmers came looking for people to harvest their crops … I was 16, wanted to get out. I guess they considered us something like Mexican workers. It was a small town and we lived in a plantation kind of shack. It was real cold in the winter—15 degrees below zero."

George Goto's family was not interned, but he cannot forget the spectre of internment that haunted his family decades after December 7, 1941.

Goto was working in a Colorado parking garage when he heard about the war. On December 8, he and his friends went down to the U.S. Custom House to enlist in the Marine Corps. "My buddies were white, and they were accepted," said Goto. "But I was rejected on the standpoint that I had a stiff finger on my hand. That was the only excuse they would give me. Yes, it was racism. The guy said, 'Well if your finger were cut off, we'd have taken you in.' I said, 'Well, if I cut it off now, could I get accepted?' He said, 'No, you got a stiff finger, you can't get in.' But racism from our friends was the worst part. Kids I went to school with turned their backs (after December 7) because I was Oriental."

The son of a Japanese father and *haole* mother, Goto may have appeared Asian to others, but he had a younger sister who was blonde and fair. "My mother told my father, 'I think we should get a divorce so that you won't be around and people won't say anything bad about Mary Lou.' So they were actually divorced after 20 years of marriage. My parents were divorced because my mother was afraid of repercussions. She heard about the internment in California and said, 'They'll get around to interning us.' So if my father wasn't living in the house, if they were divorced and if my mother got her maiden name back, they maybe wouldn't be put in a camp. They never got back together because my father passed away long ago. My mother died recently.

"To me, that's the sadness war can cause. I understood my mother's feelings, because she was afraid she and my little sister would be interned in a camp, you know, because of my Japanese father. And my father was the kind of man who would go along with anything. He didn't want to cause anyone trouble. So he said, 'Sure, we'll do it and if they take me away, it won't be a problem to you.' That's always haunted me—the fact that it was done like that."

Goto didn't learn of the divorce until he was at Camp Shelby, undergoing basic training with the 442nd Regimental Combat Team.

George Oiye was another young man who didn't learn of certain crucial events until much later. He was a freshman at Montana State College in fall 1941, having worked the previous year to earn his tuition of $55 a year. "But I saved up $65—$10 for books and that was great. I said, 'Oh man, I can make it.'"

By December 1941, Oiye had already established himself with his classmates and the school's ROTC program. Montana State College was then known for its engineering school, and Oiye, a good scholar, studied hard for a career in aeronautical engineering. December 7 changed everything. "My friends still stuck by me, but a few started picking up on the ugly pictures and the media's distortions of the truth ... I lost my American identity. I registered for the draft and never got called. I had never looked at my draft card, but it said '4-C' instead of '1-A' and I didn't know what those numbers were. And it wasn't until after the war that I understood what 4-C really was and why I had so much trouble. The problem was that 4-C meant 'enemy alien,' unfit for military service."

Such inequities were far from Oiye's mind in 1942, the year he was elected president of his sophomore class. When the college became an academy for the Army Air Corps, Oiye's friends were accepted into the program. "The Air Corps paid their way and I couldn't get in," said Oiye of the rejection. "They just weren't taking me, and of course I didn't realize that my draft classification was 4-C."

Oiye's married sister, living in Los Angeles at the time, was forced to stay at the Santa Anita Racetrack for several months before her transfer to a camp in the high desert of the eastern Sierras—Manzanar. "She told us about the conditions—the horse stalls full of manure, the wind blowing. And when they got to Manzanar, the dust was so bad they could hardly see or eat. It was just total dust. She was pregnant. And it was certainly hot at Manzanar, terribly hot."

The man destined to become Oiye's lifelong friend was in California and already in the Army, having been drafted in 1940. Susumu Ito remembered the day at the train station he said goodbye to his family. "The train came by at around 6 a.m. and here were maybe 200 *haole* soldiers and five Japanese. But there were hundreds of Japanese from the Stockton community to send us off. They soon put a stop to it—it was embarrassing the *haoles*—but this is the way the whole community felt. The Japanese felt that being a soldier was really a glorious thing, the best thing you could do for your country. They didn't say it openly but when a Japanese soldier gets killed in a war, they thought it was the most glorious way to die. It was an attitude."

Ito was out on a pass on December 7, but it soon became apparent that he should return to base camp. "They were waiting for me. They thought I could speak Japanese fluently to interrogate people being rounded up from the adjacent community of Japanese—leaders, people in responsible positions. The *haoles* accepted us in our unit but I often wondered, 'What is going to happen to us?'"

A few months later, Ito and about 200 other Japanese Americans from various camps and units were sent to Fort Sill, Oklahoma. "Indians would come up to me while I was out on pass and say, 'What tribe are you?'"

The Japanese Americans were placed in what was called "station complement," said Ito. "Which meant we had no guns, no combat duty, no training. They had me fixing trucks, while the others cleaned latrines, served as orderlies for the colonel and supplied food to the different units. And we did this for more than a year until the combat team was started."

In spring 1942, Ito's mother and two sisters were moved to a racetrack assembly center in Stockton and later interned at a camp in Rohwer, Arkansas.

Around that time, Chester Tanaka had just graduated from Washington University in St. Louis, Missouri where he received his combined B.A. and law degree by age 22

(Upper left) Shiro Kashino, Seattle, Washington. (Upper right) Ben Tamashiro, Kauai.
(Lower left) Taketo Kawabata, Kona, Hawaii. (Lower right) Roy Nakamine and uplifting friends.

and passed the Missouri bar at age 23. He obtained a pilot's license two years before. The future looked bright. The war changed everything. "The FBI came around for about two weeks, checking up on us. In 1941, I applied for the draft, but the draft board said I was an enemy alien. I couldn't find a job with law firms. They said, 'You might disrupt the morale of people and co-workers.' People in the aircraft industry said I would be a detriment. Newspapers kept asking for pilots, but I got turned down by the Air Corps who didn't want any Japanese Americans. My law classmates were all commissioned officers. So here I was, with a law degree and pilot's license and out of work. I couldn't even volunteer."

Determined to work, Tanaka eventually got a government job doing clerical tasks at a correspondents' pool. He did not know about Japanese internment until he joined the 442nd. "There was no internment in St. Louis because of its large German population, and they remembered being discriminated against in World War I. So the parents talked to their kids about it. No hatred there as in California, so I was spared that part."

Some of California's Japanese Americans weren't hit as badly as the rest. Manabi Hirasaki's family farm was left intact after his family moved to Colorado. The family was also surrounded by helpful *haole* friends.

Hirasaki, the oldest of eight children, was attending the University of California at Davis when the war started. "They notified everybody that we were going to internment camp and we had a few weeks to move out of California. But the FBI took my father, who was a visible community leader, to a place in Bismarck, North Dakota. Meanwhile, a *haole* friend and I went to Grand Junction, Colorado, bought a home there and came back for the family. Our *haole* friends took care of our farm—nothing was confiscated—and we moved out."

The political bravery of Colorado's Governor Ralph Carr made such a move possible. "Carr showed his faith by his willingness to have the *issei* and *nisei* from California relocate in his state, rather than having them incarcerated in camps," said Israel Yost, the 100th chaplain who witnessed the courage of the soldiers in Italy and France. "Because of his stand, Carr probably cut off his own political future." (About 10,000 Japanese were imprisoned at a camp in Granada, Colorado, on federal property beyond Carr's control.)

After Hirasaki settled in Colorado with his family, he was able to start school in fall 1942. "We were fortunate to have good neighbors in Colorado. And, you know, we went there because of friends, mainly *haoles*. There weren't many Japanese left."

When Hirasaki's young *haole* friends joined the Army—"and I stuck out like a sore thumb because all the young ones were gone"—he volunteered at Colorado's draft board in 1943 and passed his physical. "But they didn't know what to do with me.They put me on hold because they didn't know what to do with me. Then, suddenly, I heard about the 442nd."

Some of the Honolulu boys had a chance to bid their parents goodbye. And one of the standard types of goodbyes was from the father who said, "Do your best, whatever it is —I don't care if you come home in a coffin or not, just do your best."

Ben Tamashiro
100th Infantry Battalion

THERE PROBABLY WOULDN'T have been a 442nd Regimental Combat Team without the formation and performance of its predecessor—the 100th Infantry Battalion, composed mainly of Japanese Americans from Hawaii. Included in the outfit were about two dozen *hapa* or "halves"—for instance, Japanese-Chinese, Japanese-Portuguese and Japanese-Hawaiian.

A year before the bombing of Pearl Harbor, fully half of the 3,000 inducted men were of Japanese ancestry. About 900 of that number were volunteers. By December 1941, most of the Japanese Americans had been assigned to Hawaii National Guard (HNG) units—the 298th and 299th Infantry Regiments, consisting of Oahu and Neighbor Island troops, respectively. The regiments had been federalized and mobilized into active duty by summer 1940. After December 7, 1941, it seemed the men stood little chance of becoming an armed unit, much less the "100th."

Mitsuyoshi Fukuda was in the Big Island's Kilauea Military Camp when he was ordered to the 299th headquarters in Hilo on Wednesday, December 10. "My Army uniform was in Honolulu ... so I reported to duty in my black coat, white shirt and tie," said the man who later became a commander of the 100th.

Japanese Americans of the Hawaii National Guard and the Hawaii Territorial Guard had performed admirably following the tragedy at Pearl Harbor. (The Hawaii National Guard is not to be confused with the Hawaii Territorial Guard, the latter composed mainly of ROTC students from the University of Hawaii.) Among their duties, the soldiers strung barbed wires around beaches, constructed machine gun enplacements and guarded military installations. However, in early 1942, the War Department sought the removal of all soldiers of Japanese ancestry from active service. General Delos Emmons, commander of the Army in Hawaii, replied he had already discharged the Japanese Americans who were members of the Hawaii Territorial Guard.

"I remember when the ROTC guys were ordered to report for duty after December 7," said Harold Fukunaga, who was to become a soldier of the 442nd. "They gave us a

Springfield rifle, gas mask and helmet, and told us to guard public installations. A few months later, they kicked us out."

Wallace Nunotani, who was also a member of the ROTC at the University of Hawaii, remembered the military's fear of a land invasion by the Japanese. He was part of the personnel who guarded beaches and power plants. "At the time we were released, I was very naive to think that the crisis had passed, that they just didn't need us any more. But evidently Washington gave orders to kick us out. The next day, in a glaring newspaper headline, I read, 'Volunteers For Hawaii Territorial Guard Needed."

General Emmons left intact the more than 1,400 Japanese American soldiers in the 298th and 299th regiments of the Hawaii National Guard, plus hundreds more in the labor, service and other battalions. But their future was uncertain. "They had picks and shovels instead of guns," said Stanley Akita.

Amid suspicion against the Japanese Americans in early 1942, several community leaders of diverse races expressed support for the men. Community leader Hung Wai Ching, for instance, was on the Morale Committee under the military governor. Ching assisted the former territorial guardsmen with a petition to General Emmons. The discharged members of the Hawaii Territorial Guard formed a group known as the Varsity Victory Volunteers (VVV). Their numbers included Ted Tsukiyama, Roy Nakamine and Yoshiaki Fujitani, the son of a Buddhist minister. The men of the VVV armed themselves with picks, shovels and hoes, formed work gangs and worked at quarries, roads, warehouses and other construction jobs.

By spring 1942, authorities had been warned of a major Japanese offensive—the Battle of Midway, a turning point in the Pacific war. General Emmons worried about *nisei* loyalty if a Japanese invasion occurred. "If (war) was on this side of the ocean, they foresaw a problem," said the 100th's James Lovell. "Because they thought there would be soldiers who looked like the enemy, possibly. And who's shooting whom?"

General Emmons recommended to the Pentagon that all Japanese American officers and men in the 298th and 299th regiments be organized into a "Hawaiian Provisional Battalion" and sent to the Mainland. When General George C. Marshall, Army chief of staff, authorized the move, Emmons reorganized the Japanese Americans, and Lieutenant Colonel Farrant L. Turner, a local *haole*, volunteered to command the new outfit. Turner selected Captain James Lovell as his second-in-command. Both believed in the loyalty of the Japanese Americans. "I had taught three years at Washington Intermediate School, which was 90 percent Japanese, and more than a year at McKinley High," said Lovell. "I knew so many of them in the 100th … Colonel Turner had great faith in Hawaii. When he worked at Lewers & Cooke (a *haole* firm with missionary roots), Turner's biggest customers were contractors. Most of the contractors came from plantations, all of them Japanese. He did bonding and financing for them. Turner got to know and trust the Japanese."

Dismissed from the Hawaii Territorial Guard in January 1942, the nisei formed the Varsity Victory Volunteers and provided hard labor for the war effort.

Because no Japanese American officer was permitted to head rifle companies, Turner selected *haoles* for those posts. Among the Japanese American officers Turner selected for the 100th: Captain Taro Suzuki, Captain John Tanimura, Captain Isaac Kawasaki and First Lieutenant Katsumi "Doc" Kometani. "In a sense, Doc Kometani was the father of our battalion," said Young Oak Kim of the dentist whose stern, 'bulldog' face hid a soft, gentle nature. "He was a friend. Parents felt better when they knew their sons could go directly to Doc if they had a problem."

Some men in other outfits asked for a transfer to the newly formed battalion. Things hadn't improved since the traumatic night of December 7, when Kenneth Otagaki and Albert Oki were subjected to bodily search by their former *haole* friends in the 65th Combat Engineers. An understanding commanding officer had allowed Oki to transfer to the 298th Infantry Regiment. ("Where our buddies were," said Oki.) But Otagaki, who had a bachelor's degree in technical agriculture, found himself in the 65th's veterinary corps. "My assignment was to clean the manure from the general's riding horse … And, I tell you, I was discouraged again. I said, "Gee, if this is what I'm going to do, this is useless. So I was assigned to do meat inspection work. Although the people in charge didn't say it directly, they didn't trust me, because they thought I had a chance to poison their food, or pack something unsanitary for public (consumption)."

Eventually, every one of the Japanese Americans in the 65th Combat Engineers

(L-R) Captain Charles Brenamen; Captain James Lovell, the 100th's second-in-command; Lieutenant Katsumi Kometani; Colonel Farrant Turner, the 100th's commander. 1942.

became part of the battalion, said Otagaki. "Lo and behold, I was transferred as one of the very last to go to the provisional battalion."

The soldiers met with the commanding general at Schofield Barracks, said Oki. "He said, 'Boys, you're going overseas. You're going to be a combat unit.' There was silence. You could hear a pin drop. I couldn't think that far ahead. It didn't really set in yet."

Some soldiers, especially from the Neighbor Islands, heard differently. "Rumors were going around that soldiers of Japanese ancestry were going to be interned on Molokai," said Yuzuru Morita.

There were fears that history would repeat itself: in the 1800s, victims of Hansen's Disease (leprosy) were torn from their families and forced to live in the harsh isolation of Kalaupapa, Molokai.

On June 5, 1942, about 1,400 men of the Hawaiian Provisional Battalion prepared to sail for ports unknown on the transport ship *Maui*. "The boys from the Neighbor Islands had no chance to say goodbye to their families," recalled Ben Tamashiro of their low- key departure. "But some of the Honolulu boys had a chance to bid their parents goodbye. And one of the standard types of goodbyes was from the father who said, 'Do your best, whatever it is. I don't care if you come home in a coffin or not, just do your best.' We had no idea where we were headed for. We were concerned that we might be going to internment camps."

Around midnight, the *Maui* set sail. "Was it to be further training, POW guard detail or what?" reflected a 100th soldier. "Five days on that stinking troopship … and in its cargo hold to boot! Hot as hell. A few of us were seasick all the way. A big crap game went on day and night until we arrived on land again."

Suspicion dogged the men of the 100th. "When we docked in Oakland, California, we were practically surrounded by armed troops and herded into a separate area, troops all around us," said Oki. "We thought it was strange. It never dawned on me that we were looked upon with that degree of suspicion."

When the men, unaware of their destination, boarded their train, they were told, "Put your shades down."

"As far as I recollect, the reason given was, 'We don't want the people observing you to get all excited,'" said Otagaki. "So I was one of those guys, little by little pulling the shade up as soon as the train pulled out."

A few days later they were at Camp McCoy, Wisconsin. "The One *Puka Puka* was born," said Tamashiro, referring to the fact that the zero resembles a *"puka,"* the Hawaiian word for "hole." "One of the things I'd really like to know is why we got assigned the number, '100.' Why '100'? Maybe '100' was a distinctive number, easy to keep track of, so that you quickly know, 'That's the Japanese outfit.'"

Like the rest of his 100th buddies, Oki adjusted to the routine of basic training and enjoyed rare moments of respite. "Some of us were under the impression that we were going to combat and probably die, so the first chance we got, we went to La Crosse (Wisconsin), had a helluva time, got drunk and came home late at night," recalled Oki. "In the morning, no reveille, so we slept and slept, got up, and back at LaCrosse to have a good time."

The partying went on for several days until Jack Mizuha, their platoon leader, expressed his concern, said Oki. "Jack was a stable, clear-thinking guy who got us together and said: 'Boys, this thing has got to stop. I know we're going to combat and die, but let's die with more dignity. Think of the people back in Hawaii. It's going to reflect on them. Can you think about it?' We had family back home. That shook us up."

During training, some of the men noticed brochures that advertised, "Finish your education while training." Oki decided to do just that, and reported to his commanding officer. "I was told, 'If you want to be an officer, you have to have an IQ of at least 110,'" said Oki. "I replied, 'My IQ is 147, according to the exam I've just taken.' The officer said, 'Impossible,' and closed the book. That's the kind of treatment we got."

The military hierarchy was wrong to do that, said Otagaki. "When the war was at its height, we lost many officers—white and Japanese Americans. The officers who came from the enlisted ranks to become field commission officers proved to be outstanding."

OVERALL, THE SOLDIERS of the 100th proved to be such remarkable recruits, their record played a key role in the decision to reopen military service to Japanese Americans.

On New Year's Day, 1943, General George Marshall approved the formation of a Japanese American combat team. On January 28, General Emmons announced he planned to induct 1,500 Americans of Japanese ancestry to be trained on the Mainland and sent into combat. Under the command of Colonel Charles W. Pence, the 442nd Regimental Combat Team was activated on February 1, 1943. The response in Hawaii was overwhelming—nearly 10,000 Japanese Americans came forth. They represented a wide range of motivations—from a sincere desire to serve to leaving jobs that offered little opportunity.

Hideo Nakamine, Neil Nagareda, George Nobuo Mine and Stanley Akita were among the hundreds who volunteered from the Big Island. "My concern at the time was 'Hey, I got to do something,' said Mine. "To a certain extent my parents were resistant in that I was the only son. The other was—and this is my feeling—my dad felt why should I join the Army to fight Japan."

Mine's friend, Hideo Nakamine, saw his friends volunteering and didn't want to be left behind. There were other reasons. "I had nine brothers and didn't want them to volunteer so if anyone had to make a sacrifice in my family, I wanted to be the one," said Nakamine, who enlisted from the plantation town of Honokaa. "My oldest sister, a Japanese national, was living in Tokyo when the war started."

Likewise, Royce Higa felt if he volunteered his brothers would be spared the obligation to do so. "Unknown to us at the time, my brother Wilson secretly volunteered. All the big guns in Hawaii's Japanese community were telling us to volunteer. I thought war was glamorous. I didn't have any patriotic motive."

On the other hand, Yuzuru Morita volunteered because his two older brothers had already enlisted and "I didn't want to be left behind."

John Tsukano was 18 when he volunteered from Maui. "One of my teachers said, 'Finish your school,' and he was trying to help us, but you know how war is. Everyone gets hepped up—you see your friends go in and you want to go in."

Tadao Beppu was matter-of-fact. "I volunteered because sooner or later I would have been drafted and I was getting tired of wearing the black badge. Among the guys working, I'm the only guy wearing a black badge." Francis Tsuzuki, however, echoed the feelings of many volunteers. "I wanted to serve my country."

Royce Higa hardly had time to think after he took his physical. "They told me, 'If

Hideo Nakamine, packed gas mask in tow, poses with nephews, Kenneth and Ronnie Toguchi. Honolulu, 1943.

you think you pass your physical, come back Monday morning.' Period!" Higa reported to the August Ahrens School in rural Oahu on Monday. "They called out our names, and we never had a chance to go home. I just had my toothbrush, toothpaste, and they told us to get on the truck already. They shipped us to Schofield Barracks. It showed us that they weren't organized, plus the fact they treated us in a second class manner."

Hawaii volunteers numbered more than six times the original quota of 1,500. But the situation was different on the Mainland where Japanese Americans by the thousands were stripped of their constitutional rights and demeaned by their existence behind barbed wires. "If you were in the camps, everything taken from you, would you volunteer?" asked one Hawaii veteran. "The Mainland guys couldn't fill the quota and I don't blame them. I would have told the government, 'Fuck you.'"

TO FULFILL THE COMBAT TEAM'S requirements, Hawaii's quota was increased to 2,900 and the Mainland quota lowered to 1,500.

The resistance to inequity was particularly well organized at Heart Mountain, Wyoming, where resisters said they would be willing to serve if their rights as American citizens were restored to them.

Community leaders were ever conscious of the Japanese image and did not tolerate anything less than a united front in which all Japanese Americans were seen as proudly serving their country. Considering the way Japanese Americans were raised—"do what the government tells you"—the resistance took a certain kind of courage, said Doctor Clifford Uyeda, president of the National Japanese American Historical Society (NJAHS). "The Japanese used to say, 'Don't bring shame to the family.' Possibly the greatest stigma to a family was a criminal record. Yet, these resisters were willing to go to a federal penitentiary. Their cries for justice carried a double jeopardy—jail time from the government and disapproval from their community. The men who resisted and those who volunteered both did what they thought was right. We should honor both groups. They made their decisions based on what they thought was right, and took the consequences. This is the American way."

At Heart Mountain, Joe Hattori made his decision "right away" when he heard about the formation of a *nisei* combat team. Hattori became part of the first group out of Heart Mountain destined for Camp Shelby, Mississippi. "Twenty three of us originally volunteered, but after the Army physical, only eight of us passed," noted Hattori of the puzzling statistics. "I think maybe the powers that be didn't want us to make it. How could it be that only eight out of 23 passed?"

George Ishihara volunteered from the camp at Minidoka, Idaho. "I worked in a communications office where telegrams and other communications came in," he recalled. "So when the news came out of Washington, D.C. that we could get into the Army, we were among the first to know we could volunteer. Then and there I said, 'I'm going.'"

Shiro Kashino happened to read about the combat team in a Montana newspaper. "I felt we had to do something even though our home was a concentration camp because it would be terrible to continue to live our lives like that. The government had put us in this camp. I never thought it would do that to start with."

Many of the men who volunteered from the camps received negative reactions, said Ishihara. "Some parents said, 'You *bakatare* (stupid). You get stuck in here and you want to fight for a country that stuck you.' I didn't get that from my parents."

George Goto, rejected earlier by the Army on the grounds that he had a "stiff finger," heard about the 442nd from a family friend who was a military officer. "My brother and I volunteered and went to take our physical," said Goto. "Because of my stiff finger I thought, 'No way they're going to take me.' But my brother was rejected because of a perforated eardrum, and I went to Fort Logan. Then I took a train to Camp Shelby."

Before he ever heard of the 442nd, George Oiye wanted to be in the Air Corps like the rest of his college classmates. After he was rejected, Oiye was permitted to try again with the assistance of some understanding professors. "When I passed my physical, I was in the Air Corps as far as I was concerned. I was jubilant. And my friends and family all had a going-away party. When I got to Fort Douglas, Utah to get inducted into the Air Corps, I instead got inducted into the Army infantry. That was difficult— more rejection and this feeling of bewilderment."

Oiye was given a sealed envelope, with orders not to open it until he got to Kansas City. He opened the envelope in Kansas City. It said, "Camp Shelby, Mississippi."

"I had volunteered for the Air Force, but something unique happened. Every soldier's dog tag has a serial number that begins with a '1' or a '3.' If it begins with a '1,' you volunteered, while '3' means you got drafted. I didn't know this until after the war, but my number began with a '3.' And I volunteered. Not that it makes any difference now, but it is significant."

Susumu Ito was at Fort Still, Oklahoma, unaware of the Army's plans for him. "I hadn't heard of the 442nd," said Ito, part of a Japanese American unit at Fort Sill which had been relegated to cleaning toilets and other menial jobs. "They just grouped a bunch of us together as if we were going someplace, put us on a train and we ended up in Hattiesburg, Mississippi."

Whether from Hawaii or the Mainland, the selected men had undergone rigorous screening. They were in excellent physical condition. Many excelled in sports—from boxing, swimming and softball to football, wrestling and track. And they probably possessed the highest average I.Q. of any unit in the United States Army, according to high-ranking officials in the War Department.

On March 28, 1943, nearly 3,000 Japanese American men from Hawaii assembled on the grounds of Iolani Palace to be formally inducted into the U.S. Army. After the ceremony, the soldiers returned to Schofield Barracks in rural Oahu. On April 4, 1943,

the enlisted men rode a train from Schofield to Honolulu's Iwilei Railroad Station, then marched to the *S.S. Lurline*, a converted troop ship docked at Pier 11. "By the time we jumped off the train, the station was packed with people—friends and relatives," said Robert Sasaki. "Our departure was not secret any more."

In spite of everthing they had already done for the Territory of Hawaii and, by extension, their country, the men were treated as "less than" by the military. As they walked to their ship, their shoulders graced by flower leis, the Japanese Americans received a symbolic slap in the face: military police guarded the men along their route. "Instead of looking like proud warriors ... we must have appeared like prisoners of war being transported to some prison camp," said Daniel K. Inouye, the soldier who was to become a U.S. Senator.

The men walked about a mile under the hot sun, some of them marching with blisters on their feet. It was difficult for the Army to find comfortable fitting shoes for island youths who had gone barefoot practically all of their lives. ("They could play football and run on rocks in their bare feet," remembered a Mainland-born soldier.) Consequently, many of Hawaii's soldiers had unusually wide feet (size EEE)—a condition known locally as "luau feet." Worse, the troops were lugging 40-pound duffel bags over their shoulders. "And the damn thing was heavy," said Francis Tsuzuki. "My impression was that the Army didn't care. I was so tired from carrying the bag, yet I didn't want to fall down. All our friends and relatives were there."

Robert Sasaki agreed "we couldn't drop to the ground" with so many people around. "I remember when we left Schofield, we passed by a water tank located near a plantation. It's now a golf course. I knew a girl who lived there and she came to me with a *bento* (lunch box filled with Japanese food). All the people were standing around with *bentos* and other stuff for us. Everywhere, families and people were standing to say goodbye."

Walter Matsumoto's wife, mother and two-year-old son were in the crowd, part of the thousands of well-wishers standing on the *mauka* (mountain) side of Ala Moana Boulevard. The Matsumotos struggled to get a last view of Walter, tall and strikingly handsome in his uniform. "The men are on the *makai* (ocean) side, marching, and we were given strict orders not to break ranks," said Matsumoto, a 232nd combat engineer who would lose an eye, the hearing in his right ear and the nerves of his right arm in battle. "But my son came across, toddled across. At least I got a hug."

Matsumoto was fortunate. When the soldiers tried to wave to friends and accept a last hug from a mother or father along the route, the MPs admonished them. "Or, as in one case I witnessed, even beaten away," said Senator Inouye. "That was the farewell parade of the 442nd."

Nearly 3,000 nisei soldiers assembled on the grounds of Iolani Palace in March 1943, for their formal induction into the Army.

PART THREE

Colors
of War

Camp Shelby

The California boys came in with their 'pachuko' haircuts (slicked back ducktail haircuts), those zoot suits, those great big hats and the pants that came down tight around the ankles ... They were fancy, way out dressed and the Hawaii boys came with their bare feet, T-shirts and pidgin English. It was like throwing two roosters in a pen together.

George Goto
442nd Regimental Combat Team

ERECTED ON FORMER SWAMPLAND, Camp Shelby was an enormous, dilapidated establishment in early 1943, stretching across the lower part of Mississippi, south to the Gulf of Mexico. The initial group of Japanese American soldiers lived in company and battery "hutments" which had leaky roofs, sagging floors, broken doors, weak walls, faulty plumbing and other items in dire need of repair. "The quarters were 'chicken huts,'" observed a soldier who belonged to the 442nd's Antitank Company.

Massive repairs to the camp were done by Mainland Japanese Americans who formed the cadre, or nucleus, of the combat team. Many of the Mainland soldiers had arrived at Camp Shelby in February 1943, two months before the Hawaii men embarked on their Pacific Ocean crossing to the West Coast. The Mainland men crossed the continental United States by train to reach their base camp, as would the Hawaii soldiers who followed them. "There were between six to eight of us on our train," said George Goto, who started his trip from Fort Logan, Colorado. "The (authorities) pulled the shades down in our compartment, probably because they thought people would throw rocks at us or something."

While the Mainland Japanese Americans drilled at Camp Shelby during the day and worked as carpenters, plumbers, chimney sweeps, ditch diggers and yardmen at night, about 2,800 troops from Hawaii reached San Francisco after a five-day ocean crossing. ("I missed every meal," said Yuzuru Morita, who was seasick all the way.) From San Francisco, they traveled by ferry to Oakland, where troop trains were waiting to take them to Mississippi via several different routes—north, south, midwest. "*Haole* soldiers with guns guarded us, the *nisei* boys in American uniforms," said Oscar Miyashiro. "They took us to the train. Once we got to the train, the order was, 'Pull the shades down,' so that the people outside don't see us on the train. They might start a riot or something."

George Mine's group was also told to "pull down your shades" before they left Oakland. "Because of internment and everything else, they didn't want us to be seen," said Mine. "Could be trouble. So all the shades were pulled down. The following day, we put the shades up because we were far away from the West Coast."

George Ikinaga also remembered the orders to "keep it down, but we peeked anyway," he said. "The only time we went out was for bathroom calls at certain train stops where we could stretch our legs. It was out in the desert, nobody around for miles … I think it was done more from the viewpoint of not what we saw, but what people outside of the trains might see."

The occasional stops were a welcome relief for the men who stayed glued to their seats during most of the journey. "We couldn't change seats," observed Yuzuru Morita. "We were too obedient at the time. We just sat there."

As Mine's train headed south, he and his traveling companions received a pep talk. "I recall an officer telling us, 'I just want to let you folks know that here in the South, there are two kinds of people.' And he related to us the situation between the blacks and whites. I recall another soldier asking, 'What are we?' The officer said, 'Put yourself in the white category.' When we reached Mississippi and stopped at some railroad station, we got up to stretch our legs. I noticed that the ticket windows were labeled 'white' and 'colored.' Even the water fountains said 'white' and 'colored.' Then I realized the extent of the prejudice."

Once the men reached the town of Hattiesburg, Mississippi, convoy after convoy of trucks took the soldiers and their ukuleles, guitars and barracks bags to nearby Camp Shelby, their "home" for one year and the start of radically different experiences for the soldiers—a new environment, new cultures, new social dynamics.

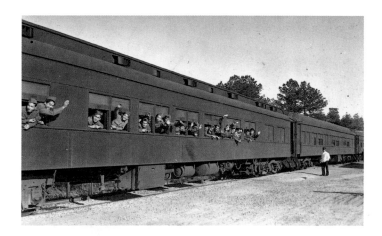

New awakenings: Hawaii soldiers arrive at Camp Shelby, April 1943, after a cross-country train ride.

(Left) Frank Seto, a Los Angeles Japanese-Mexican, was affectionately known as "Toothless" to his Antitank Company buddies. (Right) Minoru "Monk" Tateishi, Antitank Company, was known for his quarterback feats in barefoot football.

Hattiesburg was unusually cold in April, so the Hawaii men wrapped themselves in warm overcoats and blankets and huddled around stoves in their huts.

During the short period it took to process papers and assign the men to companies and batteries, the youths from Hawaii and the Mainland sized each other up for the first time.

That *haoles* filled the officer ranks was no surprise. (The 232nd Combat Engineer Company was the only 442nd outfit made up entirely of *nisei* officers and men from the start.) But there was some resentment when the Hawaii soldiers discovered that the noncommissioned officer positions were filled by the Mainland draftees who had preceded them. "Most of us were a few years older than the Hawaii boys who came, and because the core of the unit was made up of Mainlanders, there was considerable friction," explained the California-born Susumu Ito, whose mother and sister were interned at Rohwer, Arkansas. "There were significant differences in backgrounds—the volunteers who came from the internment camps and the Hawaiians. The kotonks and the Buddhaheads."

The Mainland soldiers called the Hawaii men "Buddhaheads" partly because the tanned, happy-go-lucky and beer-drinking Islanders were seen as more closely connected to their cultural roots. The Hawaii men loved their rice, fresh fish and other island foods. They thoroughly enjoyed crap games, as did people from other Asian cultures. "Only the Hawaii guys used to be in crap games," said Lizo Honma. "There were some exceptions like Frank Seto, who was Mexican-Japanese."

The term "Buddhaheads" also reflected a slurring of the word *buta*, meaning "pig"—thus, "butahead" or "pighead." In turn, the Hawaii men called the Mainlanders "kotonks." No one knows for sure how the word "kotonk" came to be. One theory says the term emerged when a Hawaii soldier knocked a Mainland Japanese to the ground. From the Islanders' viewpoint, the sound of a Mainlander's head hitting the floor produced a "kotonk, kotonk, kotonk" sound, referring to an empty head. Today, the terms are used in a matter-of-fact way by the men who became close during and after wartime. Back then, however, it seemed the only thing the Mainland and Hawaii youths had in common was their Japanese ancestry. With their different cultural backgrounds, the men viewed each other as if they came from separate planets.

"Odd, very odd," laughed George Goto heartily, when asked about his first impressions of the Hawaii soldiers. "When I first met them, I thought they couldn't speak English. They were all speaking this pidgin English. It was odd to me at first, but I got used to it."

Hawaii men were more likely to "punch you out" if they didn't like you, said the Colorado-born Goto. And the Mainland men themselves had their own perceptions about other Mainlanders, especially the ones who came from California. Goto was exposed to the California Japanese who worked the fields of Colorado in 1942, one of the few states to allow Japanese migration. "But from the standpoint of Colorado Japanese, we didn't hit it off with the California boys because they came in with their 'pachuko' haircuts (slicked back ducktail haircuts), those zoot suit jackets, those great big hats and the pants that came down just tight around the ankles. And we didn't have that in Colorado. We called the California guys 'Yoggadies.'

"They were fancy, way out dressed, and the Hawaii boys came in with their bare feet, T-shirts and pidgin English. It was like throwing two roosters in a pen together ..."

Adding to the complicated social mix were the *kibei* — Japanese who were born in America, but educated in Japan. "When they returned from Japan, the *kibei* and the California *nisei* were so different, they didn't get along either," recalled Hawaii-born Yuzuru Morita. "In general, the Mainland guys were reserved."

Japanese Americans who were born and raised in the South added another intriguing flavor. "I remember this infantryman, Yoshida, who came from Jacksonville, Florida, and spoke with a Southern twang," said Royce Higa. "We Hawaii guys laughed because we couldn't understand him at first. So we spoke pidgin with him and had a lot of fun. He was a nice guy. He was killed in Italy, toward the end of the war."

Chester Tanaka, born and raised in St. Louis, Missouri, was perplexed by it all. "First, from seeing so many Japanese, then, second, from hearing about the internment. It was a double-barrelled shock ... It was the first time I heard the word, 'da kine.' I thought they were savages. I was so bewildered. Then, I saw this distinction between the Hawaii and West Coast Japanese. I thought, 'Oh my God.'"

The sight of so many Asians at Camp Shelby didn't affect Joseph Hattori one way or the other. After all, he had been interned with thousands of other Japanese Americans at Heart Mountain, Wyoming. But he cannot forget certain aspects of the encounters

Old Glory at Camp Shelby, Mississippi

among the soldiers at Camp Shelby. "What struck me was that Hawaii people were a little on the rough side—rough in the way they talked, rough in their mannerisms. I wondered, 'What am I doing here?' And, pardon the expression, but I thought I was among a bunch of savages. That's the first impression I got."

In time, however, the easygoing Hattori discovered he fit in nicely with the troops from Hawaii. "I never drank beer until I went to Shelby. Within a week, I was drinking six to 12 beers a day. I got taught right away. I spoke pidgin so well, many people thought I was from Hawaii."

The initial lack of communication, though, proved frustrating for both sides. Yuzuru Morita recounted an early incident at Camp Shelby in which a fellow soldier from Hawaii asked for "da kine," referring to a wrench.* "But the kotonk said, 'What kind?' So we got mad. A guy from Hawaii said, 'You stupid bugga, he asked for a wrench.' I know they used to wonder about us."

Though they may have appeared brusque to many people, Hawaii's soldiers were "diamonds in the rough." They were well educated, intelligent and intensely loyal to each other, so strong were their island ties.

Virtually anything that reminded the Hawaii soldiers of the paternalistic *haole*-dominated plantations they left behind was considered suspect, observed Montana-born George Oiye. "*Haoles* spoke English a certain way, acted 'proper' (perceived as snobbish), and we happened to remind the Hawaii boys of that."

Thus, the Hawaii soldiers generally viewed the Mainland men as brought up in a *haole* way—individualistic and arrogant. In their eyes, the Mainlanders were not as group oriented, generous or happy-go-lucky as the people from Hawaii. When they visited a bar, for instance, the Buddhaheads dug into their pockets, put their money on the table and bought rounds of drinks or snacks for one another. "At first, the Mainlanders never shared things," said Morita. And if the soldiers from Hawaii didn't like a particular kotonk, "they'd yank him out of bed and beat the shit out of him," remembered George Ikinaga. For the Hawaii troops, it was a matter of "One for all, all for one," a philosophy that would prove crucial in battles—both in camp and in Europe.

"One night, a fellow in my group said or did something that offended the Hawaii guys, and I was next to him—there were some 20 or so cots next to each other," smiled Susumu Ito. "After the lights went out, curfew time, the Hawaii men sneaked in quietly and jumped this guy, and I thought, 'My God, this is terrible.' So I jumped out, started to pull the guys off, and I got pulled off. Meantime, I got beat up. But none of the other Mainlanders jumped in. They all stayed in bed. It would have been a big melee if it had

---

*"Da Kine" is a common pidgin term that translates to "the kind of," as in da kine tree, da kine house, da kine dis (this), da kine dat (that). Practically speaking, "da kine" is a convenient term that encompasses virtually everything.

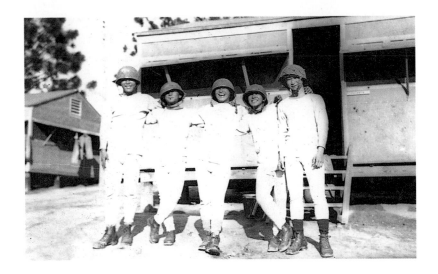

Making a fashion statement at Camp Shelby. Winters were so cold "we piled everything on our longjohns—our uniform, jacket, overcoat and then the raincoat on top of everything."

been the other way around—kotonks jumping a Hawaii man. The two of us got beat up. I had a banged head and black eye."

The antagonism between the two groups was exacerbated by small incidents that turned out to be significant in the eyes of Hawaii's men. The purchase of rice and watermelons, for example. "We asked the Mainland guys to chip in $2 a month for rice, because we wanted rice," said Royce Higa, barely able to stifle his laughter. "And the Mainland guys said, 'We don't like rice that much.' I don't blame them, because some of the guys came from places like Montana and Idaho, where they ate potatoes. The potatoes must have helped them to grow big because many of them belonged to this one company where they carried heavy weapons. But without rice, we used to get sick. When summer came, we asked everybody to chip in for watermelons. The Mainland boys said, 'We don't like watermelons.' And the Hawaii guys said, 'Everybody chip in, we got to buy watermelons.' The Hawaii guys bought watermelons by the truckload. We grew up learning to share. As a consequence, whenever Hawaii boys got into a fight they supported each other, whereas the Mainlanders would never get into it."

Because of stark contrasts between the two groups, it was difficult to communicate, explained George Oiye, who went to school with mostly *haole* children in Montana. "It was rejection in many ways, rejection by my own race. What people didn't understand back then were the cultural differences between the Hawaii and Mainland boys. In Hawaii's culture, you run in packs and protect your friends. Our culture was more individualistic, so that in itself was enough to cause friction ... Today, they say, 'How come you can sit here now and drink beer with us, when you didn't do that at camp?' I said I couldn't break through their culture."

The barriers back then were set up by a lack of understanding between the two youthful factions, most of whom were only 19 or 20. "My background was very, very (*haole*) American," said Oiye. "But it had an Eastern touch when it came to being polite, doing the right thing at the right time, saying the right things, putting your tableware a certain way, wearing your necktie a certain way. Yes, it came across as snobbish. But see, my military training in ROTC as a good soldier (dictated) that I had to be polished, hold a rifle just right, necktie, caps and flaps all right, everything polished. These things are meaningless today, but to a teenager they meant something."

Hideo Nakamine offered another insight into the complex mix of people at Camp Shelby. In Hawaii, virtually everyone was a minority. Minorities on the Mainland, he pointed out, faced an entirely different situation. "We were not afraid of the white man. But you can't blame the Mainland guys because they were abused and discriminated against by the whites, and they were afraid of coming out and fighting the white man. We from Hawaii didn't tolerate abuse. I understood how the Mainland Japanese were brought up, and I felt sorry for them because their families were in the camps behind barbed wires, and here they volunteered to join us. That's why I respect them. Some Hawaii men looked down upon the kotonks. But then we went to war and became very close."

THE MEN SETTLED INTO a dawn-to-dusk routine once they were assigned to companies and batteries. About 600 of them formed the 522nd Field Artillery Battalion.

For a while it seemed George Oiye's membership in the 522nd was not to be. He reached Camp Shelby during the month of May, alone, after most of the companies were filled. Oiye had volunteered earlier for the Air Corps while he was a student at Montana State College. He was happy at the thought of being in the corps. Once he reached Fort Douglas, Utah, however, a puzzled Oiye was inducted instead into the U.S. Army and sent off to Camp Shelby. There, Oiye was taken to see the commanding officer who informed the unsuspecting soldier of his immediate future.

"You're assigned to the 442nd Infantry Regiment."

"Hey, wait a minute, I volunteered for the Air Corps, not the infantry."

"Well, we have two other groups you may possibly get in. One is the 232nd Combat Engineer Company."

"Well, I'm an engineer. Maybe I'll go there."

"That one's full. Your other choice is the field artillery."

Oiye was stunned when he walked into battalion headquarters. "My teeth just about dropped out because I was in this whole mass of Buddhaheads," smiled Oiye. "More than I'd ever seen in my whole life … I thought they were going to send me off and fight in Japan, in the Japanese Army. I was really shocked."

Oiye was taken to C Battery and assigned to the detail section.

By summertime, the men were well into the rigors of the daily training. Like the 100th Infantry Battalion before them, the training performance of the 442nd troops was rated outstanding by the military superiors.

An August 11, 1943 news article by *Honolulu Star-Bulletin* reporter John Terry* noted of the 442nd: "We found Major Watts, 1st Battalion commander, giving instructions to his vehicle drivers. He said, 'The men in this battalion are tough. We don't drop a one of them on marches. They will march four miles in 50 minutes, carrying pack, rifle and helmet. That's about 80 pounds.'"

The men did this at the height of a humid, muggy summer in Mississippi, where temperatures often rose above 100 degrees. The heat was accompanied by a nuisance which bothered the men. "The chigger, that malevolent insect which digs its way into the skin and sets up the devil's own itch a few hours later," wrote Terry. "Sitting at the base of an elm tree, eating hot cakes, scrambled eggs, toast and coffee, and scratching chiggers, were … Hawaii boys."

To discourage the development of itchy red sores, the men used to scatter sulfur powder around or press a cigarette butt against the skin, said Royce Higa. "Chiggers buried their head into your skin, with just the rear end sticking out."

Bugs notwithstanding, the men were in excellent physical shape. Takashi Hirose and John Tsukano were among the many noted swimmers of the 442nd. Talented ball players included Tadao Beppu and George Goto. Roy Nakamine, Richard Chinen and Tsuneshi Maruo were among the outstanding boxers in the 442nd. If there was any one athletic skill that served the men well during camp, it was boxing. There was the occasional troublemaker who yelled, "Dirty Jap."

"THERE WAS SOME TROUBLE between the Japanese Americans and the all-white 69th Division," said Harold Ueoka. "When the Japanese Americans went to the post theater or the post exchange, the *haoles* would call them names and there'd be a fight. There were a lot of boxers in the 442nd, so they went and boxed the *haoles*."

When the Hawaii men fought a common foe, they were bonded by a "go for broke" spirit. Said Royce Higa, "If the Hawaii boys saw a *haole* fighting one of their guys, they'd go all out and support their friend. So there were fights all over the place."

Goto remembered a case in which a 442nd soldier stopped by the Post Exchange after attending the movies with his friends. "This kid came out, beaten up by whites," said Goto. "His friends went back to fight the whole 69th Division if they had to. But Colonel Pence (the combat team's commander) told the Japanese Americans to cool down and return to the barracks. That's why the 442nd guys were so good together during battles."

Sometimes the *haoles* didn't know any better, said Kiyoshi Takasaki. "At times,

*John Terry was killed in the Pacific during World War II.

when they called you a 'Jap,' there was no animosity, they didn't mean it in that derogatory sense. But some were prejudiced. They got beat up." (One newspaper of the time, praising the heroism of a *nisei* soldier, referred to him as "Jap Yank.")

Racism also came in subtle, unspoken forms. "We discovered the prejudice when someone found in a rubbish can a paper with the word, 'Jap,' on it," said Lizo Honma. "It was written by a lieutenant who, by the way, we never saw at the battle of the Lost Battalion. During the rescue, he was a mole who stayed at his headquarters, surrounded by rocks …"

Racial incidents were nothing new. In February 1943, a few months before the arrival of the 442nd's Hawaii troops, the 100th Infantry Battalion had been transferred from Camp McCoy, Wisconsin, and attached to the 69th Division at Camp Shelby. The 100th soldiers generally found their new locale hostile in comparison to Wisconsin, where the young men had enjoyed warm friendships with the townspeople. The atmosphere was different at Camp Shelby. "We had fights with a division from Texas because there was a lot of prejudice, no question," said the 100th's Ben Tamashiro. "There were a lot of fights in Hattiesburg. These things are all part of war."

Tamashiro and Higa noticed it was difficult for the *haoles* to pronounce their strange-sounding names. Higa's own name, pronounced properly as Hee-gah, became "High Gah." Hoshide (Ho-she-day) became "Horse Hide." And Tamashiro's name became that of a Russian general's, when he was later recuperating from battle injuries in a hospital ward.

"Every morning they'd call out the names in the ward, and this *haole* guy couldn't pronounce 'Tamashiro.' It just so happened the Russians were going great guns against the Germans at that particular time, and they had a big Russian general named Tymoshenko. The guy couldn't pronounce 'Tamashiro' so I became 'Tymoshenko' to him. Every morning, he'd say, 'Tymoshenko' at roll call. Some of the other *haoles* would say, 'Who's Tymoshenko?' Then they saw me."

Chester Tanaka was having his own problems with some *haole* officers at Camp Shelby. "They were having a helluva fun time, frequently going out 'on the town'. Their job was to censor the enlisted men's personal letters before they were mailed off. They wanted me to do it, but I said, 'That's an officer's job.' They said, 'Tanaka, censor the mail and shut up' and went to Hattiesburg and played."

Stuck with the job, Tanaka learned something about Hawaii's men, and it changed his first impression of them. "I learned that they wrote very good letters, and used fine grammar. They spoke one way, yet wrote in another way. It showed their education and high intelligence. In Hawaii, they spoke a certain way (pidgin) to understand each other. But I had not known this. Being from St. Louis, I was not around Japanese that much." (In a 1943 article, *Honolulu Star Bulletin* reporter John Terry observed, "The 442nd probably has the highest IQ of any unit in the United States Army.")

When some soldiers from Hawaii discovered that Tanaka didn't eat rice "morning, noon and night," they put him in charge of guarding the tent that held the rice supply. "The Hawaii guys traded their potatoes for rice, and this was true in Italy, where the Italians had a cuisine similar to the Japanese—lots of fish and rice," recalled Tanaka. "The boys knew I wouldn't steal the rice. Not that I was putting on airs—I like rice—but not three times a day. At night, the Hawaii men would have rice snacks. There was no *shoyu* (soy sauce), so they used the concentrated bouillion cube from their K rations. It was a poor man's substitute for shoyu. Anyway, they had me guard the rice tent."

Rice was important. Many of the men did not care for the food at the mess hall. "I'd never eaten cheese before in my life," said Royce Higa.

Whatever the adversity the Japanese Americans experienced on base, it paled in comparison to what the men witnessed during their moments away from the camp.

Soldiers on passes usually took the bus from Camp Shelby to go to town or places like New Orleans. "This black soldier got on the bus going to New Orleans," said George Goto. "The bus driver told the man, 'Nigger, don't sit there—get back in the back seat where you know you belong.' This man is in uniform and yet the driver tells him that. All the other GIs said, 'Awww, let him alone, he's a soldier.' The bus driver said, 'This bus doesn't move until that nigger gets in the back of the bus.' And I thought that was the worse thing that I had ever seen down South. He looked as though somebody had smashed his world. It was sickening, the worse case of discrimination I had ever seen up to that point."

At first, Goto and his friends didn't know which toilets and drinking fountains to use—the "White" or "Colored."

"We weren't white, but we thought, 'We'll show them, we'll use the white one,'" said Goto. "If they say anything, we'll have a fight, you know. That's exactly the way we felt about it."

In another episode, Tadao Beppu and some friends were on a bus headed toward town. They were by the station hospital. "So this black guy wants to get on, and the back of the bus is filled already. The driver says, 'Sorry, full.' Our boys said, 'Hey, what the hell the difference. One more guy's not going to break the bus—let 'em on.' So the poor guy got on. He was begging because his wife was coming in on the train from Detroit, and if he wasn't there to meet her, she'd be lost. So he was begging …"

Roy Nakamine was returning to Camp Shelby from Jackson, Mississippi, when the driver slowed down to pick up another soldier. "Then the bus driver took off," said Roy. "I looked outside and saw a black man. I remember thinking, 'If that was me, I could miss my pass deadline and get punished for that. That soldier was returning to camp from a pass. I thought, 'What will happen to him?' and felt badly for him … Those days, there was no excuse for being late."

During that era, "colored" civilian employees traveled to Camp Shelby in a special

"added on" back section of the bus. "The front was for white employees only," said Stan Akita. "When the bus stopped, the back door opened, and only blacks got off."

Sometimes the Japanese American soldiers were outraged enough to throw their driver off the bus. "In one case, the driver had actually kicked a black GI off the bus with his feet, so one of our guys beat up the driver," observed Akita. "This 442nd guy had been drinking beer—he was feeling good and getting mad at the same time—and beat up the bus driver."

Requests for peace came from Colonel Charles W. Pence, the combat team's commander. "Always the colonel comes, and always a meeting, meeting, meeting," said Oscar Miyashiro. "Sometimes the people from Hattiesburg complained that we were riding with the blacks in the back of the bus. So the colonel said, 'You sit in the white section, the colored are in the back.' But once we saw an empty space in the bus, the Hawaii boys just sat down wherever. We didn't care. We weren't prejudiced like that."

Soldiers of African ancestry routinely had a rough time virtually everywhere they went, said Kiyoshi Takasaki. "The blacks were all segregated—I would say they were in a division of about 12,000 to 15,000 troops—and what bothered me most was that they couldn't get into town because they could only ride in the back of the bus, and only about 10 could go on the bus at any one time. So most of them walked that 15 miles or so to town. The sad part was the fact that the black division was not from the South. They were from the Midwest—Indiana, Illinois, places like that. So it really must have hurt them."

Manabi Hirasaki shook his head at the memory of an encounter at a Hattiesburg bus stop. "There wasn't a prejudicial thought in my head—we're all people," he said. "I was talking to a black man and he asked, 'Could you buy a hamburger for me?' I said, 'Why don't you go in and get it yourself?' and walked away, without realizing what I had done. I didn't know (the situation). We were 18, 19, 20 years old at the time. I thought, 'Here's a grown man, he can get his own hamburger.' But he could not. He couldn't go to the counter because it was reserved only for whites. Restrooms and everything. I look back and feel bad about it, but I didn't know."

Susumu Ito also remembered Hattiesburg decades later when he visited South Africa, where the differences were even more striking. "There, people were segregated in three groups—Europeans, coloreds and blacks—for the use of bathrooms, train stations and so forth. So I asked my host, 'Where do I go?' I was thinking of Mississippi. To give you an example of the hypocrisy, my host said, 'Sus, no, no, no, you go into the white areas.' They said, 'You're an honorary Caucasian.' I asked, 'How about Chinese?' They said, 'No.' The whole thing was ridiculous."

Yuzuru Morita noticed "a strange thing" during his stay at Camp Shelby. "When blacks and whites worked together, like a road gang, they worked well together and talked to each other. But when the whistle blew for lunch or to quit working, the blacks went to one side, while the whites went to another."

(Left) Earl Finch offered his hospitality to nisei soldiers in Mississippi. Finch was royally welcomed in Hawaii after the war. (Right) Colonel Charles W. Pence, 442nd commander, was well-liked by the men.

Col. C.W. PENCE

Varying degrees of racism could be found virtually everywhere in the United States, but confronting it in such an overt way startled George Ishihara. "When we went into Hattiesburg, blacks didn't walk on the same side of the street. We went into a bus depot and saw restrooms for blacks. I personally didn't experience (racist) remarks, but the Hawaii guys got into a lot of fights on account of that. They didn't take guff from anybody."

The soldiers had been warned. Senator Daniel K. Inouye remembered the bright, sunny morning he and his fellow members of E Company stood in formation awaiting inspection. Captain Ralph Ensminger, the company commander, stepped onto a raised platform and read a directive. "We were ordered to observe the laws and customs of Mississippi as they related to race relations," said Senator Inouye. "(Captain Ensminger) said, 'You may not like it, I may not like it, but that's the way they do things here and that's the way it's going to be...Much of this will rub you the wrong way but I am asking that you abide by it ...' It was noticeable to us that Captain Ensminger was choked with anger.' You men have an additional battle to fight (later). You have to overcome the prejudice that will be thrown at you.' This second battle (racial prejudice) will occur after the war." (Captain Ensminger was one of the first casualties of the 442nd. He died on the first day of battle in Italy.)

The men of the 442nd kept their thoughts and feelings inside for the most part. "It was something that was accepted at the time," said Joseph Hattori. "It was beyond our power to change it so when we sat in the back of the bus on purpose, we were making a statement."

Some *haoles* were also making a statement. One, Earl Finch, is remembered fondly by the Japanese American soldiers for his hospitality and kindness. The soft-spoken Southerner, in his 20s, often invited some of the men to his farm for home-cooked meals prepared by his elderly mother. Finch also made sure that the soldiers received fresh fish from time to time. "He flew it out to camp," said Shiro Kashino. "I remember eating sashimi. He brought watermelons for the boys. He really did like us."

There was the time when Finch invited Richard Chinen of the 442nd's headquarters company and other Japanese Americans to experience something new—a "possum hunt." The outing was described by newsman John Terry through Chinen's words: "We went off into the woods on horses. We had a hunting dog. He did a lot of barking, but we never got the 'possum. Mr. Finch said the red fox scared him off. I never had so much fun in my life. That day out at Mr. Finch's was the first time I ever heard hog calling, and what I mean, the hogs came running. They came from everywhere. Mr. Finch told me to tell the boys to come out to his place any (time). I told him, 'Someday you come to Hawaii, and we treat you Hawaiian style.'" (It was a promise kept. After the war, Finch visited Hawaii and the soldiers returned his kindness in full measure. He lived in the Islands until his death at age 49.) In 1943, Finch's kindness toward the Japanese Americans brought the FBI to his door.

DRILLING, TRAINING AND SPORTS occupied the men's days and nights at Camp Shelby. The 232nd engineers, for instance, learned how to detect mines, clear roads, construct bypasses and destroy bridges. "When the bridges were blown up, we constructed temporary bypasses," said Walter Matsumoto of a dangerous job where speed was crucial. "We tried to build them as quickly as possible and make them passable enough so that jeeps, weapons carriers, small vehicles could deliver supplies to the men when they dug in for the night."

Members of the 522nd spent long hours with their 105 millimeter howitzers (the guns have a seven-mile firing range) and learned the fundamentals of surveying, forward and aerial observation, directing fire, communications and more. "The nerve center is at headquarters battery—radios, telephones, and where the fire direction center calculates the powder charge to use, the setting of the gun barrel in terms of compass direction as well as what they call 'sight angle,'" said Don Shimazu of Headquarter's Battery. "Through the communications system, the message gets through to all the gun batteries— A, B and C. Each battery has four gun crews, four guns, and they're all separated by some distance, so they can't be yelling at each other. By telephone, each gun gets the same message."

All of the 442nd's supporting units—Headquarters, Service Company, the 522nd Field Artillery Battalion, the 232nd Combat Engineer Company, the Antitank Company, Cannon Company, the 206th Army Band—learned how to best sustain their infantrymen, the soldiers most directly in harm's way.

232nd Engineers construct a pontoon bridge in minutes.
Camp Shelby, July 1943.

Part of the infantry's training was captured by reporter Terry, who described the scene almost prophetically. Fourteen months before the 442nd soldiers became immortalized in the now legendary Lost Battalion rescue, Terry wrote: "Moonlight flooded the meadows with a pale light, and cast dark shadows through the pine woods. There were soldiers everywhere—three battalions of them. The woods were literally full of them. But you seldom saw them … Moonlight, silence and the unseen presence of hidden troops made it seem unreal. The only persistent sound was the whirring of locusts in the treetops … We noticed a group of men … walking Indian fashion across a moonlit meadow. They were the heavy weapons company of the battalion. They moved out from a group of pines, filed across the meadow and vanished into the dark woods beyond … In the moonlight, their soundless movements … seemed ghostlike."

The men were training intensely in summer 1943, when the U.S. Army's Military Intelligence Service (MIS) sent recruiters to Camp Shelby. The intelligence corps had done this several months before when it went to Camp McCoy, Wisconsin, during the Thanksgiving weekend of November 1942, and plucked about 70 men from the 100th Infantry Battalion.

Again, at Camp Shelby, recruiters sought Japanese American troops proficient enough in reading and writing the Japanese language to serve as translators, interpreters and interrogators. They became part of the 6,000 Japanese Americans in the MIS. Many of them were *kibei*, Japanese born in America but educated in Japan. Together, the *nisei* MIS proved to be extremely valuable throughout the Pacific—from Alaska, Hawaii and China to the Philippines, Japan and Australia. Some MIS soldiers, originally with the 100th or 442nd, left their buddies reluctantly.

"I purposely flunked the MIS recruitment test because I wanted to stay with the 442nd," said Ted Tsukiyama, who eventually served with the MIS in the China-Burma India theater. "But they must have looked at my record and learned I attended Japanese language school. So I involuntarily went to Camp Savage, Minnesota, in August 1943 for training. We were ordered not to tell anyone what we were doing."

For a brief, happy moment during the summer of 1943, the men of the 100th and 442nd enjoyed a reunion among relatives and friends at Camp Shelby. When the Hawaii soldiers of the 442nd first arrived at Camp Shelby in April, the 100th Infantry Battalion was away on maneuvers in Louisiana. (The 100th was transferred earlier from Camp McCoy, Wisconsin to Camp Shelby in January 1943.) Now, as they shared news about home, the men also bid each other goodbye: the final group of (MIS) Japanese language interpreters was leaving for their training site at Camp Savage. The 100th's Donald Kuwaye was not expecting to be one of them.

"In July 1943, (a month) before the 100th shipped to North Africa, a special order came for me from Washington to be sent to MIS training," said Kuwaye. "Alone, I rode a train from Mississippi to Minnesota. Ultimately, I went to China." (Kuwaye later

Liberty in New Orleans: (Standing, L-R) Edwin Honda, Roy Fujii, Robert Imura, Dunn Yamauchi. (Kneeling, L-R) Edward Nakamura, Masami "Joe" Takata.

preserved much of the 100th's history as editor of its publication, *The Puka Puka Parade*.)

The 100th Infantry Battalion itself was preparing for an Atlantic Ocean crossing and the European battlefronts. Roy Nakamine, a 442nd soldier, was among them. "I volunteered to go with the 100th," said Nakamine of a unit that engaged in battles so fierce, it would require numerous replacements from the 442nd. "I remember we left in August 1943, because August 20th is my birthday."

While soldiers of the 100th were distinguishing themselves as the "Purple Heart Battalion" in Italy, the 442nd was in Mississippi getting "combat ready" to join them.

In November 1943, for instance, the 522nd was in Louisiana on maneuvers with the 69th Division. The battalion began acquiring a reputation as "sharpshooters," to be sure, but there were also moments of play and strange encounters.

George Mine visited a barbershop in a small town. "The barber asked, 'Where did you learn to speak English?' recalled Mine. "Again, this shocked me as a kind of humorous thing."

Another time, the Hawaii soldiers, yearning for fresh food, spotted something interesting. "We saw an armadillo burrowed in the ground, its rear end sticking out," said Royce Higa, who was typical of the Hawaii soldiers who sought fresh food whenever possible, such as fish, cows and chickens. "So we ate the armadillo. It tasted like chicken."

The weather turned icy cold and snowy during maneuvers. The men slept in tents and learned to be innovative. "We stacked wood from the pine trees, covered them with branches and laid on top of the whole thing to be above ground," said Higa. "I remember I had a wood tick, which had been in my belt buckle on my stomach, sucking the blood. We weren't able to take a bath for a long time."

As the combat team trained, soldiers of the 100th in Italy were hit by a high number of casualties and needed replacements. Stanley Akita, Oscar Miyashiro and Wilson Higa were among the 210 men and 20 officers sent by the 442nd to the 100th in February 1944.

"Wilson came to me before he went overseas," said his brother, Royce, who had just returned to Camp Shelby from the Louisiana maneuvers. "He came to say goodbye. I knew he was going to die. I just knew it. I had $40, and gave it to him."*

During training, some of the 442nd soldiers visited a concentration camp in Jerome, Arkansas. "One of my friends in our battery wanted to visit his Japanese language schoolteacher and her husband, who had been a doctor in Hilo," said Harold Ueoka. "That place was located on nothing—empty space, no houses, just empty land, no nothing. The

*Sergeant Wilson Eiki Higa, the son of Kama and Ushi Higa, was killed in action near Antonio and Anzio, Italy, April 26, 1944.

people were put in barracks, surrounded by barbed wires. At the gate, guards stopped us. We stayed at Jerome over the weekend with a family who made room for us ... We ate with the family. I understand the doctor used to make $19 a month. How come they put the Japanese in those camps (by the thousands), and not the Germans and Italians? This is my personal question."

George Goto had no idea of the prisoners' conditions until he visited Jerome one day with a 442nd buddy. "People were living in little bitty rooms in the barracks, separated by a sheet. I couldn't imagine anyone living like that. My friend said, 'I can't stand this no more,' and we left."

When Ueoka and Goto visited Jerome, one of its many internees was Hawaii-born Ruth Oekawa Ishimoto. Shortly after the attack on Pearl Harbor, the FBI paid a visit and her father was taken away. "I've blocked that part out," said Ishimoto.

But "someone from the federal agency" returned. "The condition was, we would also go to the Mainland and be reunited with our father."

Ishimoto, her mother and 15-year-old brother traveled on the *Lurline*, a converted troopship, in December 1942. "The families with babies really had it rough," she recalled. "When we got to Oakland, soldiers with machine guns were at the train doors. And like prisoners of war, we went into the camp."

Ishimoto was one of several women who belonged to a camp USO to bolster the morale of the homesick Japanese American soldiers at Camp Shelby. They gave dances, cooked Japanese food, made gifts and wrote letters to the men who were already overseas. Mary Kochiyama was one of the many dedicated individuals who lifted their spirits. "Mary and Earl Finch did all they could to help the boys," said husband Bill Kochiyama, who volunteered for service from Topaz, a concentration camp in Utah. "After we went overseas, Finch sent Mary to Minnesota to form the Aloha USO for the Japanese American soldiers training with the MIS."

There was no doubt that the 442nd, like the 100th that preceded it, was in remarkable shape and ready to ship out. They had been training for nearly a year—from spring 1943 to spring 1944. "The 100th took basic training about four different times and went on maneuvers three times," recalled George Goto. "And we in the 442nd had done basic training twice and took maneuvers, because, you know, they didn't know what to do with us and we were the best trained troops they had. The 100th did so well, they said, 'Give us the rest,' and sent the whole combat team over."

Before the combat team was sent overseas, General George Marshall visited Camp Shelby. "I remember General Marshall came to see us on a Sunday, a day which was usually a holiday for us," said Royce Higa. "Maybe for security reasons, they didn't want anyone knowing that we were headed overseas."

That morning, General Marshall reviewed the combat team, and left as abruptly as he arrived. When Colonel Charles Pence, the 442nd's commanding officer, announced to the men that the general was pleased by what he saw, a lieutenant muttered softly, "Well, that was the kiss of death."

Royce Higa remembered the last weeks before the men shipped out, and the system of internal security that operated at Camp Shelby. "They asked a few of us on the base, 'Are you ready for combat?' 'How do you assess your group?' 'Do you notice any weak links?' 'Any hesitation?' In retrospect, it was quite an unusual procedure."

On April 22, 1943, the 442nd headed for its staging area at Camp Patrick Henry in Virginia. Ten days later, at Newport News, Virginia, the soldiers walked up the gangplank of their *Liberty* ships at night, calling out their first names as a checker at the pier called their last names. Some of the soldiers could hardly be seen beneath their heavy packs and large helmets.

Higa wasn't among the crowd. He and a few other soldiers broke out with measles and had to stay behind, becoming part of the 171st Infantry Regiment. (The 1st Battalion was left behind as a cadre for replacements, and eventually became the 171st, which trained most of the replacement troops for the 442nd.)

Higa's friend, George Ikinaga, can still visualize the moment the 442nd left the United States to confront the unknown. He and thousands of other Americans sailed silently over the dark waters in one of the largest gathering of ships ever to leave Chesapeake Bay—more than 100 strong. "When we left Newport News, we had only one ship going out," said Ikinaga, who traveled with hundreds of his buddies in the hold of a small, slow-moving *Liberty* ship. "Next morning, you could see nothing but ships from one horizon to the other. Convoys. I recall someone saying, 'This is one of the largest convoys going across.' This was done to protect us from German U boats. From one horizon to the other, nothing but ships, ships, all ships, as far as the eyes can see ..."

General George Marshall reviews the polished troops of the 442nd. Camp Shelby, March 1944.

Home Fire

These haole *soldiers from the Mainland looked at us and couldn't tell the difference. They were probably thinking, "How come these POWs are wearing American uniforms?"*

Edward Tarutani
1399th Engineer Construction Battalion

DURING THE TIME that their friends and relatives in the 100th/442nd were training on the Mainland or fighting in Italy and France, Japanese American soldiers in Hawaii were coping as best they could. "We followed closely the troop movements of the 100th/442nd, wondering how long the war was going to last," said Edward Tarutani. "We worried about them."

Tarutani was one of the more than 1,000 Japanese American men who served with the 1399th Engineer Construction Battalion. (Soldiers of the 370th Engineer Battalion inducted prior to February 1942 comprised the nucleus of the 1399th, which was officially activated in April 1944.) They labored day after day under the hot sun and completed more than 50 major defense projects on Oahu during the war, including the construction and maintenance of roads, bridges, ammunition storage faciltities, barracks, airfields and more. They also built three jungle-simulation training sites where more than 300,000 soldiers became familiar with jungle warfare. Behind these projects were men with thoughts and feelings about this difficult time in their lives.

Shiro Matsuo, who had a brother in the 100th, remembered how it was in the beginning when the men worked under the ever-watchful eyes of their military superiors. "When the 442nd was activated and they asked for volunteers, sad to say, many of our boys were disillusioned already. You can't blame the boys. They had been treated like dogs, doing all the menial jobs. We didn't have passes. We didn't have rifles. No training. No rank. No nothing. Some of us were supposed to go with the 100th, but the military (didn't have) laborers and that's why we were kept. We were under the jurisdiction of whatever outfit that needed us. So our boys went up to the rock quarry, dug ditches, cleaned up rubbish. At that time I was in charge of the latrines. When I told my mother that, she wanted to die."

The men, recalled Matsuo, were constantly followed around by *haole* soldiers with rifles. "At this rock quarry, a *haole* sergeant said, 'Bust that rock.' That first time, I

Duke Kawasaki and his 1399th buddies share a rare break. "The 1399th men worked like dogs. They rose in the morning, stuck out their hands and got a shovel or a pick."

weighed only about 107 pounds and carried a 16-pound sledgehammer. When I hit that rock, the vibrations went gongggg, I shook, and everybody laughed. I was okay, but there's a skill to busting a rock. We had no training. That's the scary part. We never dreamed we'd go into the Army and be in the rock quarry. That stuff is for prisoners."

The troops in the 1399th were indeed treated like "cast-off spare parts," wrote Roland Kotani in *The Japanese in Hawaii: A Century of Struggle*. "(They were) issued uniforms which didn't fit, constantly harrassed by noncommissioned officers and assigned to do dirty ... work ... The U.S. Army had demonstrated little appreciation for these Americans of Japanese ancestry."

Harold Yokoyama wondered about that too. "Were the men in the 1399th outcasts? Why couldn't they have guns? When I was given a gun, there were no bullets. I said, 'Where's my bullet?' But nobody said anything, nobody protested. I had a gun, no bullets, and guarded tanks and stuff in the dark."

In addition to suspicion, racial prejudice dogged the men of the 1399th, just as it did the 100th/442nd. "Our boys were on a truck and *haole* soldiers were yelling 'Jap, Jap' at them," said Matsuo.

Tarutani recalled seeing Japanese, German and Italian prisoners of war held at a camp on Oahu. "So these new soldiers from the Mainland looked at us and couldn't tell the difference. They probably thought, 'How come these POWs are wearing American uniforms?'"

But there were some *haole* military men who looked beyond the superficiality of race. "They found out we had skilled artisans in our outfit—carpenters, engineers, skilled guys," said Matsuo.

Yokoyama suspected as much. "In 1944, they drafted Japanese Americans to replace people in the 442nd. A friend and I requested combat, but they wouldn't let us go. We had carpenter skills ..." (The 1399th included a future actor, Harold "Oddjob" Sakata of "Goldfinger" fame.)

Meanwhile, Matsuo was "discovered" by a *haole* mess sergeant who removed him from latrine duty and placed him in the kitchen. "He told me, 'Learn to cook.' He was from Minnesota. We got along fine with this company of inductees from Minnesota. This mess sergeant was nice to me. I said, 'Someday, I'll take care of this *haole* boy.'" (Matsuo, who went on to open a successful chain of restaurants, fulfilled that promise in 1984 when he invited the sergeant and his wife to Hawaii, all expenses paid.)

Matsuo and Tarutani jogged each other's memory as they conversed about their wartime duty decades later. "We slept in barracks," recalled Tarutani, who began service with the 1399th in 1944, two years after Matsuo.

"You guys slept in a building, we had a shack."

"We sometimes slept in tents."

"Our toilet was a hole in the mountain."

Camaraderie and humor helped the men to survive their daily grind back then; however, the 1399th did not escape tragedy. "One of our boys was hitting rocks when a chip flew into his eye and blinded him," said Matsuo. "In Kahuku (rural Oahu), the military was doing maneuvers with an airplane via remote control. The plane slammed into this dump truck from the rear and killed two of our boys instantly—Sergeant Jack Miura and PFC Susumu Motonaga. Another time our dump trunk fell into a ravine, crushing one of our boys. You didn't have to go to war to get killed."

There were many incidents like that, said Tarutani. "I remember this guy was repairing a tire—we had little safety protection in those days—and the tire blew its rim, which hit his head. I was nearby, so I held onto his head—it was open and he was bleeding badly—but luckily he survived. Another time, I happened to look up in the sky when I saw two Air Force planes on maneuvers collide. I don't know why, but I thought of the soldiers in the 100th/442nd and could only imagine what they were going through…"

Central Pacific Base Command patch worn by men of the 1399th.

100th/442nd Campaign Highlights

NAPLES-FOGGIA
September 9, 1943 to January 21, 1944

The 100th Infantry Battalion. Action at Salerno, the Volturno River crossings, Cassino.

ROME-ARNO
January 22, 1944 to September 9, 1944

The 100th fights at Cassino and Anzio from January 1944 to June 1944, before reaching Rome. The 100th becomes part of the 442nd Regimental Combat Team at Civitavecchia, Italy in June 1944. In late June, the 100th/442nd moves northward along the Italian coastline. Among the towns: Suvereto, Belvedere, Sassetta, Rosignano (Hill 140), Leghorn, the Arno River, Florence. (From August 15, 1944 to September 14, 1944 the Antitank Company is temporarily detached from the 100th/442nd and deployed as a glider unit in Southern France.)

RHINELAND
September 15, 1944 to March 21, 1944

The 100th/442nd arrives Marseilles, France in late September. In October 1944, the soldiers fight at Bruyeres and Biffontaine; rescue the "Lost Battalion" in the Vosges forests before reaching St. Die. The unit is sent to the French Riviera from mid-November 1944 to March 1945: the Maritime Alps, Sospel, Nice, Menton.

CENTRAL EUROPE
March 1945 to May 1945

The 522nd Field Artillery Battalion is detached from the 100th/442nd in early March and moves through southern Germany. Among the sites: Rhine River, Worms, Heidelberg, Augsburg, Dachau, Munich. Occupation duty in or nearby Donauworth, Germany.

PO VALLEY
April 5, 1945 to May 8, 1945

Main body of 100th/442nd moves from France to northern Italy, late March 1945. Landmarks, as the unit fights northward: Massa, Carrara, Genoa (by the Ligurian Sea), the Po River.

● Paris

FRANCE

Dijon ●

Lyon ●

Marseilles ●

Toward the Purple Hearts

And sadly do I realize
The plight of many a soul as I
Be born to live, to suffer, die,
Unseen, unheard, unknown, unknelled;
Like chips upon a checkerboard,
No choice, no will, resigned, compelled.

Masayuki "Spark" Matsunaga
From a poem he wrote while recovering
from wounds in a hospital, Naples, Italy,
December 1943

BY THE TIME THE 442ND set sail for Europe in April 1944, its predecessor, the 100th Infantry Battalion, had been fighting in Italy for eight months. The 100th's overseas tour began when it reached Oran, North Africa in September 1943. "We thought, 'Where are we going? What are they going to do with us?'" said Major James Lovell, the 100th's second-in-command at the time. "Then we learned we'd be in combat, not just guarding troop trains. See, the Arabs were stealing things on the trains. They'd steal our guys' duffel bags, cut holes in them, put their legs in and pull the bags up around them. So some of our guys saw Arabs going down the street with Japanese names on their backside."

The 100th was attached to the Fifth Army's 34th Red Bull Division, commanded by Major General Charles W. Ryder and composed mainly of men from the Midwest—Iowa, Minnesota, Nebraska and the Dakotas. ("The Buddaheads pal up with the Bull Heads," noted a 100th soldier.) The 34th Division, the first American division sent to Europe at war's onset, was recuperating in North Africa after its African campaign. On September 19, 1943, the 100th left North Africa and headed for Italy.

The men landed on the beachhead at Salerno on September 22, 1943. On September 29, Sergeant Shigeo "Joe" Takata, B Company, was hit in the head and face as he advanced toward an enemy position on a rainy, muddy day. Takata became the first rifle-carrying Japanese American to die in combat, the first of the 100th to receive a Distinguished Service Cross. "Joe's death still sticks out in my mind," said Roy Nakamine, a 442nd soldier who volunteered to go with the 100th when the battalion left Camp Shelby. "I was shocked, the first *nisei* to die in battle. Reality set in. This was no longer training."

From October to November, men of the 100th crossed the chilly, waist-deep waters of Italy's Volturno River three times. "(The following) happened when the 100th crossed the Volturno River and had its first encounter with the Germans," wrote Chester Tanaka in *Go For Broke*, his 1982 book. "It was about 4 a.m., and as they crossed the river, the entire front line yelled, '*Banzai*,' and the Germans all let their guns down. They just stopped fighting … They were shocked to see Japanese Americans on the Italian front, fighting against them."

The hills around the Volturno were heavily mined. "The Jerries were out of sight and you didn't know when you were going to meet them," said Nakamine.

Hill 600 was especially brutal. Yoshinao "Turtle" Omiya, second platoon, D Company, was crossing the Volturno for the third time, moving single file up the hill through thick olive groves. "I was on the lower part of the hill, the fourth man in the formation, when our messenger Alekoki happened to trip a 'Bouncing Betty,'" said Omiya, whose lieutenant was Masayuki "Spark" Matsunaga.* "The irony was that the ones who stood directly under the umbrella of the explosion were not touched. But those of us on the outskirts were not so lucky. Yasuo Kawano, our walkie-talkie operator, was killed. Sparky got hit on the leg. And you know what happened to me."

Steel fragments of the exploding "Betty" punctured Omiya's right eye, shattered it, leaving his left eye "dried up" from the concussion. Omiya was blinded for life. Kenneth Otagaki was one of the many 100th soldiers who were there.

"Turtle was all banged up, Spark's injuries weren't as severe, so I told Spark, 'I'm going to get the others first,'" said Otagaki. "He said, 'OK, OK.' … You should know this. For every Congressional Medal of Honor, for every Distinguished Service Cross, there should have been many, many more. How do I know? I was a litter bearer, and I used to go up front and pick them up. And nobody in the back knew what the hell went on in the front. These are some of the things people don't know. If you were up at the front and said, 'I did this' or 'I did that,' no one would believe you. The Congressional Medal of honor and other medals were often given if you knew the officers and had enough good write-ups."

There were many unsung heroes, soldiers who did not receive the Purple Heart because they believed their own injuries were minor in comparison to the severe wounds suffered by their friends.

Isaac Akinaka was a medic and religious man who volunteered for everything, day or night, said Otagaki. Try as he did, Otagaki couldn't seem to get away from his Good Samaritan friend. "Akinaka would pick me all the time, and I got so mad at him. I'd say, 'Isaac, pick on somebody else—I'm tired.' And we'd go back and forth like this:

---

*Spark Matsunaga served as Hawaii's United States Senator from 1976 until his death in 1990. Turtle Omiya died in 1984, shortly after our interview.

(Left) Kenneth Otagaki, a medic with the 100th in Italy, was a University of Hawaii wrestling champion. (Right) Yoshinao "Turtle" Omiya, with Audrey, his see-ing-eye dog. ("She also rolled over on her back when I took a sunbath.")

"Don't worry Ken, God will take care of you."

"God will take care of me? God might take care of you, but He won't take care of me because I'm not a devout guy."

"Don't worry. I'll go in the front of the litter. I'll take care of the bullets and everything."

"But they might come from the side."

"Don't worry."

Akinaka grabbed the front of the litter, Otagaki grabbed the back, and Akinaka ran. "He literally dragged me and I'd say, 'Not so fast, not so fast.' I could hear the bullets coming. I said, 'Hey, I'm going to go down.' He'd say, 'Don't worry, those guys need us.' Men like Akinaka, in my opinion, should have been given the medals. They went way beyond the call of duty."

The 100th's Albert Oki can testify to Akinaka's "go for broke" efforts. "I was earlier wounded on Hill 600, where Sparky and Turtle got hurt," he recalled. "And Akinaka picked me up and carried me down … I remember at training camp, while we were carousing and roughing it up, Isaac would be sitting in a corner reading his Bible. We looked at him and thought, 'What kind of guy is this?'"

Roy Nakamine was another example of the kind of soldier Otagaki was talking about. Nakamine's experience was typical of many others who experienced extreme dangers but who remain unknown to this day. Only after prodding, did the soft-spoken Nakamine talk about his tour in Italy. "I remember four of us carrying the wounded, making our way through mine fields. We worried more for the wounded than ourselves. I don't know why we thought like that. But we didn't want the wounded to suffer even more. So we were careful walking through the mine fields. We saw people doing even more than we did, but they never got medals. I remember a fellow with the 100th who led a whole battalion up a hill loaded with mines. He'd place toilet paper to mark the mines. In my opinion, he should have gotten the Congressional Medal of Honor."

In mid-January 1944, just before the fighting at Cassino, Otagaki himself was hit by shrapnel. He and six others were part of a patrol that had volunteered to rescue a wounded soldier. "You can't abandon your friends," emphasized Otagaki. "You just can't abandon your friends." When a mortar shell struck the patrol, the explosion killed three and wounded three others, including Otagaki. The former wrestling champion of the University of Hawaii lost his right leg at the hip, his right eye, two fingers from his right hand and a chunk of his chest. "When I saw Ken in the hospital, he was comatose," said Albert Oki, his buddy. "His rehabilitation was so severe and painful."

Israel Yost, the 100th's chaplain, remembered the evening the men were killed or wounded. "That was one of the worst nights I ever had."

THE REMAINING SOLDIERS of the 100th continued their northward drive, taking every given objective. They faced blizzards, mud, rain and Germany's crack SS troops at Cassino. So severe was the fighting, some of the 100th's platoons were reduced to only three men. For the men of the 100th, Cassino would forever become "Purple Heart Valley."

From late March through May 1944, the soldiers were at Anzio, a 10-mile square Allied beachhead which was subjected to awesome German firepower—from rockets and aerial bombs to machine gun fire and a huge railway artillery gun. Here, the 100th helped to set the stage for the breakthrough to Rome.

The battalion took a key pass, when two other regiments failed to do so. "Some questions had arisen in the minds of certain officers and one asked General Ryder, 'If six battalions couldn't take that pass, how can you expect one battalion to take it?'" remembered Young Oak Kim. "The general said, 'I have other regiments ... but I don't think they can do it. I know the 100th can take the pass.' The next day, we took the pass."

The 100th's Charlie Diamond, born in Yokohama, Japan, was remembered by friends as a "lovable Japanese Hawaiian who carried his rifle, his equipment and always his guitar." Italy, 1943.

General Ryder noticed something else about the gutsy soldiers: they loved fresh food, wherever they could find it. Cabbages, burdock roots and an ox, for instance, made *hekka*, a Japanese dish. There were other improvisations. "I knew some of the men were throwing concussion grenades into the river to catch fish," said Kim. "And such use of grenades was forbidden by all rules and regulations. So I investigated to see how many fish they caught. I saw General Ryder approaching from the other direction and we arrived at the spot together. For a few seconds, the men didn't realize he was there. When they saw him, they were standing in the middle of the stream with their mouths open. Floating down the stream were dead fish. General Ryder said, 'What's that green stuff those men are picking in the water?' I said, 'That's watercress.' He said, 'Do you eat that?' I said, 'Yes, that's a great delicacy ...' He said, 'I know the men miss their seafood, and the Oriental vegetables. I'm sorry I can't do anything about that, but I have ordered that all the rice that comes to the 34th Division will be diverted and sent to the 100th."

Between Anzio and Rome, in the area of Lanuvio, Tamotsu Shimizu volunteered to go on a mission with several other 100th troops to retrieve bodies of their comrades. Shimizu, hurt twice before in combat, nevertheless chose to return to the front after hospital recuperation. The men were unaware that the Nazis had wired the dead soldiers with booby traps which exploded when the bodies were moved. "The guy on the left bent down to pick up one leg, and I did the same—that's all I remember until I regained consciousness," said Shimizu in a 1979 *Puka Puka Parade* interview with Ben Tamashiro, the 100th's historian. "I tried to get up and wondered why the hell I kept falling on the ground, toward my left. Then I looked, and here was my left sleeve without an arm ... Others were hurt too." (At the evacuation hospital, someone wondered out loud if Shimizu was a 'Chink' or a 'Jap.')

Hawaii soldiers sought fresh and familiar food. They pickled vegetables, Japanese-style, in their helmets. Once, a soldier tied a chicken to his back. The enemy fired. When the smoke cleared, he saw only string and floating feathers.

"Hey, kotonk, I get da chicken—you get the Kraut!"

Captain Young Oak Kim (left) reviews 100th's Honor Guard at Leghorn, Italy, with the Fifth Army's General Mark Clark and Undersecretary of War Robert Patterson.

On June 5, the day after Shimizu was injured, the 100th's weary soldiers could see Rome and looked forward to entering the welcoming city. Much to their disappointment, however, the 100th was not to be the first American battalion to roll into Rome. The troops were ordered to halt and wait for truck transportation, while other units made a victorious entrance into a city filled with cheering people.

Technically speaking, an armored division was supposed to be first, said Young Oak Kim, but it stopped periodically when faced with the enemy. "We deployed our infantry, the Germans backed off, the division proceeded, then waited again for us. We unplugged obstructions for them about five or six times. The division could have just plowed ahead, but didn't. Knowing the master plan, Rome should have been cleared hours earlier. It was a disappointment (about not entering Rome first), but we were not assigned that task."

The 100th reached Rome that evening. "People probably wondered, 'What are all these Chinese doing here?'" said Lovell. "Because Italians would say, 'Chinese, Chinese.'"

The decision to hold back the 100th was a question mark, said John Tsukano, who had joined the battalion as a replacement from the 442nd. "The 100th made the breakthrough. They spearheaded the breakthrough. But the Army stopped the 100th from entering Rome the first day. Whatever the reason, it was a big blow because the men worked so hard."

The 100th moved into an area near Civitavecchia. With about 900 casualties by that time, the battalion's original strength of some 1,400 men was reduced to less than half. Soon, the Buddhaheads from Hawaii would meet kotonks from the Mainland and more Buddhaheads from Hawaii. Ships carrying the 442nd were nearing the Italian coast.

"Why do you fight for America?"

An Oriental fellow came by, slowed down and glared at us, just stared at us. We looked at him, thinking, "Why is he in German uniform?" He looked at us as if to say, "Why are Asians in American uniforms?" Then we realized the German guard was a young Japanese.

George Nobuo Mine
Prisoner of War

"WHEN WE GOT TO the Mediterranean, I looked around and thought, 'Hey, where's all the ships,'" said George Ikinaga. "I felt like a loner."

After nearly a month zigzagging across the Atlantic Ocean, the ships carrying the combat team entered the narrow entrance of the Mediterranean one at a time. On June 2, 1944, most of the soldiers walked off their *Liberty* ships. Some of the men wobbled down the gangplank, exhausted and seasick.

They were at the war-ravaged harbor of Naples, located on the west side of Italy. The combat team's 2nd Battalion had earlier been dropped off at Oran, North Africa, only to be placed on another ship to Naples to rejoin its unit. Some of the 522nd Field Artillery Battalion soldiers reached port at Brindisi. Meanwhile, another group of 522nd soldiers docked at Bari, on the east side of Italy, and backtracked by train to Naples only after a "comedy of errors."

"The captain of the ship was telling the crew, 'Put the anchor down,' but he was going in pretty fast and the crew didn't understand the instructions or something and they didn't get the anchor down," said George Oiye, C Battery. "And we were all lined up with our duffel bags, ready to get off, because we saw the pier coming up. And then we smashed into the pier, people went flying, duffel bags fell into the water, the ship went all over, and we banged into the harbor wall."

Whether at Bari or Brindisi, the men got on a "rinky dinky cattle car," said Ikinaga. "I think Hawaii's plantation trains which hauled sugarcane were in better shape. The wheels were so small, I don't know how they went."

The men rode to Naples on "40 or 8" box cars, so named because the stinky freight trains were capable of hauling forty men or eight horses. "It was so cold, we tore up the floors on the box cars, put them on fire, and here we were on this flaming train whizzing by," said Oiye. "Before we got off the train, a whole bunch of kids came up and starting singing 'Rum and Coca Cola' to us. I was flabbergasted. Here, we were, practically burned up from that flaming train, and then the kids singing, 'Rum and Coca Cola.'"

Like countless other soldiers before them, the men of the 442nd witnessed the extreme toll of war, especially on the children. "Mothers were hustling their daughters, brothers hustling their sisters—the whole family had to survive that way," observed Ikinaga. "If the (Italian) boys saw a cigarette butt, there'd be a mad scramble, since cigarettes were a big luxury for them. Kids would hang around dump sites, carrying gallon cans to pick up food leftovers from the dump."

It was rare to find a cat in Italy, remarked Walter Inouye. "Lots of rats, but no cats."

By the middle of June, the 442nd soldiers caught up with the 100th at Civitavecchia, north of Rome. The 442nd was attached to the Fifth Army's 34th Red Bull Division; the 100th became a part of the 442nd, taking the place of the 1st Battalion which had been left behind at Camp Shelby. The 100th, an extraordinary fighting unit, was permitted to keep its distinctive number.

Sergeant James P. O'Neill, a correspondent for *Yank*, a weekly Army publication, observed the summer 1944 reunion in Italy. "For three days, the brass hats left the two outfits alone. The kids of the 442nd plied their older brothers with questions of war. The older brothers, like all combat men, dodged these questions and asked about Hawaii, their families and girls. Together, the outfits visited Rome, buying souvenirs and baffling the Romans, who decided they must be Japanese prisoners. It was impossible for them to believe these were tough, loyal Americans … After three days, the men of the 100th began to answer the questions of war … and in the evenings, they would sit together and drink *vino* and sing their soft Hawaiian songs."

Like the seasoned troops of the 100th, the 442nd's soldiers learned quickly that the reality of war was unlike the logical theories of books and manuals. Susumo Ito, a forward observer, remembered the first moments he headed for the front in Italy. "As I walked with the infantry, the farmers would come out of their houses and pour red wine for us. I remember getting pretty darn drunk. It was so hot—that hot sun, and these people coming out and greeting us."

Lieutenant Walter Matsumoto's introduction to war was something he never forgot. "Before we hit the town of Suvereto, we engineers moved in a convoy of trucks. We were up in a hill on the right side. When we looked toward the left side of the valley, we saw the infantry moving in columns, what was called a 'squad column.' That was done according to the book, but pretty soon you find out it doesn't work in combat. You have to go with what the ground affords you. We saw the infantry getting busted up the first day from 88 millimeter enemy shells."

Both sides eventually paid a steep price for the 442nd's objectives of Belvedere, Sassetta and Castagnetto. "(The Germans) pushed the 442nd out of the valley and pinned the soldiers ... in an exposed and highly uncomfortable position in a wheat field," wrote O'Neill. One enemy gun was hitting F Company especially hard with direct fire. Private First Class Kiyoshi Muranaga volunteered to destroy the 88 milimeter gun with mortar fire. His third round landed directly in front of the enemy's position, but before he could fire again, the German gun crew located Muranaga and killed him.

The 100th, which had been held in reserve, attacked through the middle, between the 2nd and 3rd battalions. Their drive cut off the enemy's retreat lines, freed the 2nd and 3rd battalions, took the high ground above Belvedere and left the SS troops in shambles. Meanwhile, B Company's 1st platoon prevailed in the town of Belvedere, after fierce house-to-house fighting.

By the time the supporting units went along a road traveled previously by the infantry, the damage was there for all to see. "The first thing I remember is seeing a lot of dead Germans by the road, bodies, but we couldn't stop," reflected Hattori. "Then I saw the first Japanese American soldier by the roadside ..."

Because the soldier might have been a friend, Walter Inouye turned away whenever he came across a body in American uniform. "I saw instances where Italians tried to steal things from the bodies."

With the 2nd Battalion held in reserve, the 100th and 3rd battalions took control of Sasseta. For the soldiers from Hawaii, pidgin played an important role in confusing Germans who happened to be eavesdropping as the Japanese Americans chatted on their walkie-talkies. For instance, "Hama hama Tommy gun boltsu, hayaku eh? And ammo mote kite kudasai" was a simple "hurry" request for a Tommy gun bolt and ammunition. But the Germans didn't understand the strange talk.

SOUNDS OF PIDGIN and the fresh foods of home were to become sheer fantasies for George Mine and other Japanese American soldiers for it was near Sasseta that Mine, A Battery, 522nd Field Artillery Battalion, became a prisoner of war.

Mine was the driver for a forward observer team, headed by Lieutenant Edwin Wood, which was relieving another team at the front. "I happened to have the only jeep available so I got assigned to driving Lieutenant Wood and his team to the front to meet the 100th's Captain Kim," recalled Mine.

The team members reached their rendezvous point at dusk, ate dinner and moved forward again. Lieutenant Wood and his radio operator walked with Captain Kim, while Mine's jeep kept pace between the infantrymen who flanked both sides of the road. They reached a point where the jeep could not go any further because the road had been rendered impassable from heavy shelling. Mine was instructed to return to the rendezvous point and join the lieutenant the next morning. "I was roused from my sleep

(Left) George Mine, at Camp Shelby, months before his capture by Germans in Italy, summer 1944. (Right) Sassetta, where Mine began his life as a POW.

by Captain Kim's driver and we both went out and passed the road, which was now repaired. There were three jeeps headed for the front—Captain Kim's driver was ahead, I was in the middle and the driver for B Battery was in the back. We came to a top of a knoll, overlooking the village of Monteverde, when I noticed an infantry unit on the left having breakfast. I learned later when I returned from the war that the infantrymen thought, 'Who are those crazy guys going down that road?'"

Mine saw no guards posted, nothing to warn the drivers that they were headed into a village full of Germans. "As we drove into the valley, the driver of Captain Kim's jeep rounded a turn and disappeared behind the hill. When I came through the hill, I heard a rattling sound, metal or something. At least that's the impression I got. Then the jeep conked out, wouldn't move. I looked up—I had dust goggles on—and saw someone in a greenish uniform firing away at my jeep. He motioned for me to come out with my hands up. I thought he looked Italian. Then I realized he was a German soldier."

When Mine left the jeep with his hands up, he heard firing again and thought the bullets were destined for him. The German soldier was shooting instead at B Battery's jeep driver, who had been traveling behind Mine. "The driver saw my hands up, so he reversed his jeep, weaving backwards until it too conked out. I could see him running and ducking into an Italian's farmhouse. I wondered, 'I hope he did not get hit.'"

During the few seconds that the German soldier was firing at B Battery's jeep driver, Mine took a good look at his own jeep. "He had raked a section of my jeep and water was running out. I heard the rattling when he fired at the jeep. Fortunately, I had a sandbag under my foot, on the jeep floor, so the bullets went on the side. My feet were above, on the sandbag. At that point, you don't think about those things."

As Mine was taken toward the Italian farmhouse, he saw a jeep in front and an Italian woman carrying a baby. When the German soldier asked about the other driver, the woman replied, "I don't know." Mine looked up at the two-story house and wondered if he'd run upstairs and hidden. "I later learned he did run upstairs and that he was ok."

Mine was marched off the road, from its bank into a quarry. "I thought, 'This is where I'm going to die.' Another German searched me and took this brand new watch I purchased just before I left the Mainland."

When they reached German headquarters, Mine realized he had company—expected and unexpected. "I met eight guys from the 442nd's F Company who were captured the night before. Some of us were held by the entrance area near the gate, where German soldiers were walking back and forth. An Oriental fellow came by, slowed down and glared at us, just stared at us. We were kind of curious too. Here was another Oriental, you know, but he wore a German uniform. He looked at us as if to say, 'Why are Asians in American uniforms?' And we looked at him, thinking, 'Why is he in a German uniform?' We didn't know he was Japanese until a guard said something like, 'Watanabe.' A guy in F Company answered. But the German wasn't looking at him. The guard was looking at this other guy. Then we realized the German guard was a young Japanese. See, the Germans conscripted a lot of Japanese students who were attending college in Germany during wartime. They'd been drafted by the German army."

The men were kept together until they got to Bavaria—"someplace around Munich." Within 10 days of the jeep incident, Mine found himself in Stalag 7A, in Moosburg, Germany. "I was there for about two or three months. Then they segregated us. I was a corporal at the time, and the noncommissioned officers and privates were separated. The privates were sent to work somewhere in Germany. We were sent to a noncommissioned officers' camp. From there, we were shipped by train to a place known as Furstenburg on the Odor River to Stalag 3B. The Odor is a river that channels north to south, and is on the east side of Berlin. I was there for about four months. Following that, we were marched west because the Russians were closing in so fast. We marched from the camp on a ten-day, forced march of 100 miles, sleeping in barns, warehouses, schoolhouses, as we moved from place to place."

DURING MINE'S IMPRISONMENT and migrations, the 100th/442nd itself was moving quickly, taking every given objective. They engaged in ferocious fighting against Germany's tough Wehrmacht units, helping to clear the approaches to Leghorn, Pisa and Florence. By the time the unit's role in the Rome-Arno campaign was over, the combat team had suffered nearly 1,300 casualties to gain 40 miles of Italian countryside. That casualty figure represented more than one-fourth of its total troop strength. General Mark Clark of the Fifth Army was reluctant to let go of the Japanese American unit. (He would get them back six months later, when the Japanese Americans returned to Italy to do what others could not—break the Germans' Gothic Line.)

The 100th/442nd landed in Marseilles, France, on September 30, 1944. After the unit was moved by trucks or trains up the Rhone Valley, the soldiers settled briefly in an assembly area near Bruyeres under the command of General Alexander Patch's Seventh Army before their unit was attached to the 36th Division.

There, the Japanese Americans faced Germany's awesome firepower—from heavy artillery to rocket launchers. The area was extensively mined, especially the surrounding Vosges Forest. Hidden machine gun nests interlocked with other invisible machine gun nests in the dark woods. Nevertheless, the soldiers liberated Bruyeres by mid-October. During the last week of October 1944, they entered one of the most dramatic battles of World War II—the rescue of the 36th Division's 1st battalion in the Vosges forests.

The 100th's Stan Akita, Roy Nakamine and Oscar Miyashiro were among the 100th's soldiers who would never see the Lost Battalion. They became prisoners of war at Biffontaine, just a few days before the rescue attempt. "We didn't know what was going to happen day by day, but it may have been a blessing in disguise," said Akita retrospectively of their frightening capture by the Germans.

Akita remembered the evening of October 22, 1944, when two men were sent out to contact the ration patrol. "We hadn't eaten all day and the men were eyeing the rabbits and chickens running around. We had captured a German ration wagon, horse drawn, but found only a pot of soup and the famous German Army bread which had a content of 23% wood pulp. Since we were not accustomed to eating wood pulp, we gave all the food to our (27) German prisoners who were very pleased. That night we took turns guarding the prisoners and during my watch, I gave them a few cigarettes to pass around. We also gathered hay for their beds and overall we treated them very nicely." (The acts of kindness would be reciprocated, as Akita and the others later learned.)

The two men who had been sent out returned with baggy eyes early the next morning, October 23. They told the commanding officer of their encounter with many Germans in the hills and that they barely made it back to headquarters. "I had a very queer premonition something was going to happen to me," said Akita. "It was a belief up the front line that the longer you go without a scratch, the harder you'll get hit and I had already spent eight months without a scratch ... I know of guys who got wounded in battle, got out of the hospital and returned with more wounds. These are the guys with the four, five and six oak leaf clusters on their Purple Heart medals."

Akita reported to his commanding officer, saying he would rather not be on the patrol that took the prisoners back. Even Sergeant George Hagiwara had a feeling something would go wrong. "I went to the commanding officer and told him I didn't want to lead the patrol," said Hagiwara.

Young Oak Kim, Chicken Miyashiro, Sam Sakamoto and Roy Nakamine were among the wounded who were being evacuated. Nakamine was hurt in the ankle. Kim, hit in the palm of his hand by machine gun fire during a house-to-house fight at Biffontaine, lost a lot of blood and was dazed from the pain-killing morphine.

Akita and Hagiwara were part of a detail of soldiers who had to take German prisoners back to battalion headquarters. The detail consisted of 11 medics, who carried no weapons; six wounded litter cases; four walking wounded; and six guards. German prisoners served as litter bearers. "It was spooky in that dark forest," said Hagiwara.

"About 9 a.m., Sergeant Tokunaga and an English-speaking Jerry reached the top of a knoll and what they saw could have made anybody pee in his pants," recalled Akita, who recorded his experiences in a diary shortly after the war. "A company of about 150 Jerries was sitting, lying down, 'chewing the fat.' Thinking fast, the sergeant told his prisoner to ask the Jerries if they wanted to give up and go to America. It seemed they were tired of fighting because half of them threw down their weapons, but the officer in charge, a true Hitler man, had some of his men surround us."

What happened next became a blur. Hagiwara, Kim and Richard Chinen, a medic, took off into the bushes. "The rest of us who didn't know the situation yet figured the three men were backtracking to find a trail," said Akita.

Kim, woozy from morphine, felt like he was floating. "The medication had a strange effect on me. I lost my sense of time and distance."

Nakamine was limping along in the rear, when he saw Kim and Chinen whizz by. "I said, 'Where're you going?' but they didn't say anything. I think they had the idea that if everybody tried to escape, no one could escape. But at least some escaped to relay information and get help. But when they came back, we were gone—captured."

The tables had turned. The Japanese Americans were now prisoners of war. "The Germans had been waiting for us—they had their machine guns mounted," said Oscar Miyashiro. "Somehow I feel they knew we were taking that trail."

Heavily guarded, the prisoners marched with their captors, heading closer to Germany with each step they took. "It seemed like a bad dream from which I couldn't get up," said Akita. "After realizing we were actually prisoners, my morale was so low I felt it tickling my toes."

Akita watched his guards closely, observing the human face of war. "The front line Jerries in my opinion were gentlemen. They never took anything from us except our arms. I had a Parker pen and they left it alone. Even our (superior) American cigarettes were left alone; When they saw us tiring under the weight of the litter, they gave their guns to their comrades and relieved us. Once, when the Jerry officer stopped at a farmhouse for directions, we saw a vegetable patch with tomatoes, beans, cabbages and more. We pointed at our mouths to show we were hungry. The officer pointed at the vegetables and told us to get some. I never did like tomatoes raw, but it sure tasted good then. Even the cabbage tasted good, flavored with bouillon cubes melted in a little water. It reminded us of home where raw sliced cabbages and *shoyu* were common."

When the men emerged from the forest near a small town, the able-bodied prisoners were separated from the wounded and herded into a barn. A guard entered at dusk, giving the men a few loaves of "that 23% wood pulp bread," said Akita. "Hungry as we were, we couldn't stomach that bread. It was the same size and shape as our American

(Left) Stanley Akita. In 1972, he sought and found his former prison in Strasbourg. (Right) Ex-POWs Oscar Miyashiro (right foreground) and Roy Nakamine (top row, second right), happily join their buddies for the trip home.

bread, but it weighed almost two pounds and was very hard. You could kill a guy if you hit him on the head with it. We stayed up late, talking about food we used to eat back home—*sushi*, fresh fish cooked with *shoyu* and sugar. We felt full just by swallowing our saliva."

The following morning, the prisoners were herded into a vacated shop in town and kept there for a few days. "Our food got a little better at the shop," remembered Akita. "Dinner consisted of two slices of meat, bread, a few leaves of lettuce and soup."

One night the German officers interrogated the men, two by two, in a dimly lit room. What did Buddhism teach? What did they learn in Japanese language school? And why were the Japanese fighting so hard for America, the German officers wondered. "Because of the democratic way of life—everybody is free," said Akita.

"Do you feel like an American?"

"Yes."

"Did you know a cat born in the fish market isn't a fish?"

"Yes, but he belongs to the fish market."

The next day, the prisoners were transported to a French village near the German border. They stayed in a small section of an abandoned textile mill. "It looked more like an overgrown dog kennel," said Akita. "We ate, slept and relieved ourselves in that room ... The following day, the 17 of us were loaded onto the back of a truck which looked like the dog catcher's wagon you see in the comic books."

Children from a small village yelled and waved their hands. "We threw them a few candies and they scrambled for them like chickens for worms," observed Akita.

The longer they traveled, the older the German guards appeared to be. "One night, our guard was an old man of about 60, with graying hair and teeth missing from here and there in his mouth," said Akita. "Food of the day was thin soup and the UGH! 23% wood bread ... The cold was the most miserable. It was teeth-shattering cold. We had no blankets. All we could do was pile about six excelsior mattresses over us, and yet it felt like sleeping in an ice box."

At some point, the hungry and tired men were marched to Colmar, near the French-German border. The absence of small luxuries such as cigarettes had become critical, said Akita. "After the cigarette was smoked to about one-half inch of the butt, we'd put out the fire, salvage the tobacco and save it in a container. After we got enough tobacco, we'd make a cigarette out of newspaper and smoke it."

At Strasbourg, another border town, they entered a large brick building encircled by barbed wire and were led to the fifth floor. "This was the first time, since becoming a prisoner, I felt we were really entering a prison," said Akita. "Glancing down, we saw Polish cooks who were prisoners themselves, showing us cigarettes. We tore up a burlap bag mattress cover, tied a nail to the end and lowered it four stories. They tied two Pall Mall cigarettes. We were really surprised to receive American cigarettes from a Polish prisoner."

After a few days, the POWs rode on a train to an old cavalry camp in Stuttgart where they were housed in a horse stable and received their first American Red cross food parcel. Said Akita, "Actually, one prisoner was to get one parcel a week. But due to lack of food, a prisoner could eat it in two or three days and starve the other four. By now, our rations from the Germans were pretty set. Breakfast was a cup of 'coffee' that tasted like our local *habu cha* (tea). Lunch was a bowl of thin barley soup. Dinner was four to six boiled potatoes, a slice of that 'sawdust' bread and an occasional thin slice of sausage. The Red Cross parcel consisted of five packs of cigarettes, one can of powdered milk, one candy bar, one can margarine, a can of meat or fish, a package of M&M candy, a package of crackers and a box of diced fruits ... A most revolting thing happened to us the first day. We noticed two wooden barrels in the corner. It was used for your daily business. That day they brought our soup in two containers exactly like the two in the corner. That first serving of soup didn't sell so good ... We were interrogated again—about Buddhism, whether we liked America and so on."

French and American prisoners continued to trickle into the stable. Finally, the men were placed on a cattle car painted with the words, "10 Horses or 50 Men." It was so cold at night, the prisoners slept side by side together, facing first to the right, then to the left, turning whenever one got tired of sleeping on one side, said Akita. "When we had the chance to relieve ourselves (outside), we would pick up as much wood as possible and get temporary heat by burning the wood in our steel helmet."

After a train ride of several days, the prisoners ended up at their home for the next six months—Stalag 7A, a camp about 45 miles northeast of Munich. "It was a huge camp of about 20,000 prisoners of war from all the allied nations you could think of," said Akita. "It was surrounded by a double barbed wire fence and machine gun towers. Every fifty yards, there was a sentry on foot accompanied by a German police dog. If a POW came too close, the dogs just growled and showed their fangs. The first night was spent in a barn with no floors. It was infested with fleas and bedbugs. Our bed was a bundle of straw spread on the ground. And sanitary conditions were terrible."

Each man hung on to his margarine can, a "lifeline" for their precious coffee and soup. One tap outside the building was used to wash their cups and spoons. Especially memorable was "delousing," when the prisoners' clothes were placed on racks, pushed into an airtight vault and sprayed with gas. The naked men waited for almost three hours, said Akita. "It was a very uncomfortable feeling standing naked, with no pockets to put your hands into. Just picture 200 men not knowing what to do with their hands. After retrieving our clothes, we were led, to our dismay, right back to the flea-infested barn."

Though they started off staying in the same compound, the Japanese American POWs became separated in time. "I noticed Stan ended up with *haole* Americans, and Roy was with French prisoners," said Miyashiro, who was imprisoned with other Japanese American POWs.

POW camps seemed to be one place in which the privates and PFCs were a little better off than the officers, noncoms and medics, regardless of rank, observed Akita. "By the Geneva Convention rules, the privates and PFCs were the only ones the captors could use for work detail."

Work detail meant rising at 4:30 a.m., riding for about two hours on a cattle train to Munich and clearing the rubble within the city or by the railroad. However, work detail also gave the POWs a chance others did not have. "If the guard was good, he'd let us trade our Red Cross cigarettes for bread or potatoes," said Miyashiro. "A loaf of bread was about three cigarettes."

This bread had no sawdust in it, was softer and could be sold back in prison for even more cigarettes, said Akita. "We privates who could get extra loaves were rich. The best trading I had ever done was the time I had nine loaves of bread. The pockets inside of our overcoats could take care of 10 loaves. I was elated. I could just picture the eight packs of cigarettes ... One of the best work details was the potato digging detail. We'd shovel spuds in the wheelbarrow and fill our overcoats with them at the same time. My partner and I had fried potatoes, mashed potatoes, boiled potatoes and potato soup. Potatoes were running out of our ears."

Besides food and cigarettes, work detail provided the POWs unforgettable sights in Munich. "I saw Jewish prisoners," said Miyashiro. "They had striped uniforms on. I can't recall their condition. I also noticed Russian prisoners who were starving, really skinny, because they didn't have the Red Cross parcels like we did."

A train pulled up one day when Akita was working on the railroad. "There were literally thousands of crying babies—only babies on the train, with nurses running around in there," he said. "Later I learned that young German men training to become officers—intelligent, physically fit—were at a camp a few kilometers away from the young nurses. They were encouraged to intermingle ... So the train was filled with boy babies. I saw this train. The guard told us, 'These are boy babies, they got rid of the girl babies.'"

In another instance at Munich, Akita saw a Japanese youth dressed in a German guard's uniform, a sight POW George Mine witnessed months before in Italy. "At first I thought he might be Mongolian, but this one really looked Japanese. He was young. The Mongolians who worked in labor battalions were older."

The Japanese Americans themselves aroused curiosity from the civilians, noted Akita. "They'd ask the guard if I was a Chinese soldier. When they were told we were Japanese, the people had that 'How come?' expression on their faces."

Sometimes a "Good Joe" guard allowed the men to remove their underwear and bury them in the snow for an hour, remembered Akita. "Later, we'd just shake the snow and pick off the frozen lice and fleas."

Roy Nakamine used to go out on detail but not daily, he said. Like his friends in other compounds, Nakamine shared similar experiences. He made soup out of potatoes, secretly exchanged cigarettes for food with the German guards at night and learned to sleep with fleas. "Every night we'd fight with the fleas. We couldn't take it at first, but after a while we got used to it."

During his imprisonment, Nakamine witnessed a sight he cannot forget. "I saw Jewish prisoners—I don't know what they were doing—walking outside, stooped, shaggy, old," he said. "The other prisoners looked halfway decent compared to the Jews I saw. Then one time in Moosburg, I went to the infirmary and saw nothing but Jews who were too weak to walk. So the Germans called us to transport them from the hospital to, I think, a truck. They were nothing but skin and bones. I hated to see that. I felt so badly for them. I think they were being sent to Dachau. Moosburg is close to Dachau, a few miles away, although I didn't know that at the time. Some of my fellow prisoners in our compound discussed that they had seen Jews being placed in a big building, like a warehouse or showers. When I saw movies and read books later, I thought, 'So that's what they were talking about.'"

Nakamine, a medic who had walked through mine fields in Italy to rescue the wounded, held within his heart another item he would not think about until years later. Like many other injured Japanese American soldiers, he left his evacuation hospital during wartime to be with his friends at the front. "Remember I told you I had a concussion in Italy during the early part of the war and got sent to a hospital? I was feeling OK and went out on a one-day pass to the front line. I stayed there for seven days. My friend, Captain Katsumi Kometani (the 100th's medical officer) said, 'Are you OK? You'd better get back or you'll be AWOL.' When I got back, an officer questioned and court martialed me and put the AWOL on my record. That one black mark is still there. I returned to the front line because I wanted to be with my friends. I told the authorities, but they didn't believe me."

NAKAMINE, MIYASHIRO, AKITA and the other Japanese American POWs never got to see George Mine during their imprisonment at Stalag 7A. By the time they arrived in late October 1944, Mine was gone, transferred north to a camp by the Odor River—Stalag 3B. ("Near Frankfurt on the Odor River," said Mine. "We were there about four months.") With the threat of advancing Russians—"the Russians sought revenge for the slaughter of their civilians by the German Army"—their frightened guards hurriedly marched Mine and the other prisoners west to a camp at Luckenwald, Germany—Stalag 3A, about 26 miles below Potsdam. "We were evacuated into circus tents—no barracks available—with hay on the floor. About 500 of us in one tent. Latrines were not available so they dug an open pit with no covering or anything.

"One night the British bombed Potsdam, and the echo at night made much louder sounds than bombings during the day. The whole place shook up ... So you couldn't find any space by the latrine pit because everybody was standing around that. If the bombs came closer, everybody would have dived into that toilet pit. Next morning, you see slit trenches all over the place because people were digging with whatever they had—digging foxholes."

Life in Mine's camp became a matter of just surviving from day to day, he said. But he was also observant and careful. "There was a German sergeant who acted naive. To me he was play acting. Americans sometimes got overconfident and thought the sergeant was dumb. But Germans raided the barracks on occasion and pinpointed a cache of food supplies, cigarettes and other things."

There were moments of psychological escape. Longtime prisoners included talented schoolteachers, musicians and other professionals. "So they created theater in which they produced plays like *Oklahoma* and *Show Boat,* if I recall correctly. The men acted in women's roles. There was stage lighting—dim lights, bright lights, flashing lights. Prisoners were doing this."

Mine slipped into the familiar delousing routine since the prisoners slept in flea-infested hay. Once, he happened to be in the front of the line, which was guarded by an elderly German. "Well, this American soldier friend of mine, Anderson, spoke fluent German. The German guard looked at me, looked at my friend and asked, 'Japana'? My friend replied in German, 'Yes, yes, the Japanese soldier is now part of the American Army.' And the German guard looked at him, looked at me and shook his head because to them, the Japanese were allies of Germany. He couldn't understand."

As the POWs waited for something to happen, they thought of families, friends and home. "We wondered, 'When is this war going to be over?'" said Oscar Miyashiro. "We were hoping the rest of the unit was OK." The POWs had no knowledge of the Lost Battalion rescue in France. "I wondered about my friends," said Roy Nakamine. "What was happening to them?"

PART FOUR

"I Can
Never
Forget"

I was put in Dachau for many months. On that afternoon, this Japanese American came and saved my life. I was on the ground, couldn't walk ... If the war had lasted another day, I would not have lived through it. I was on my last breath. I drank some caraway soup. Up to that time, I felt alone in the whole world.

Josef Erbs
Survivor of Dachau Concentration Camp
April 1945

THEY WERE IN THE MARITIME ALPS of southern France from November 1944 to March 1945, guarding an 18-mile front along the Franco-Italian border. The 100th was ensconced by the Riviera, the 3rd Battalion was situated in Sospel, and the 2nd Battalion was in the frigid high slopes of the Alps. Their severely depleted ranks needed rest and replenishment, having suffered an inordinately large number of casualties in Bruyeres and at the epic rescue of the Lost Battalion. No longer could the 100th/442nd be used as a regiment-sized force.

Though the men dubbed their time in southern France as the "Champagne Campaign," they still suffered casualties. Only their combat team stood between the Germans at the border and Marseilles to the west, so there were occasional hit-and-run skirmishes. Soldiers sometimes ran into mines on their frequent patrols. Pack mule supply teams plodded on steep, dangerous ridges to and from isolated mountain outposts.

With its glistening coastline, Menton was the scene of at least one bizarre incident during the men's "Champagne Campaign." A squad of the combat team's Antitank Company was observing the harbor. "When we saw the dome of a submarine approaching, heading inland," said Donald Nakamura. "It came too close and got stuck in the sand. The German inside the sub is motioning us to push him back in the water. He didn't want to open his sealed dome, so 'Fiduke' Yokoyama took a screwdriver and loosened one screw of the dome. The German opened the dome right away and stood up. We were surprised."

In spite of such surprises and dangers, the men's eyes lit up decades later when the conversation turned to this particular time and place in their lives. "That's when our group ended up going to Menton (by the Riviera), and oh, that duty was so go-o-o-o-d," said Neil Nagareda. "We were in this sanitarium with beds. We couldn't believe it—beds, you know, and hot meals. It was a king's mansion. Menton was big and beautiful."

Here, the soldiers were far from the gloomy forests which had been deeply stained with their blood. With passes in hand, they headed for the sunshine, wine and laughter of Antibes, Cannes and Nice. Some of the "Go For Broke" soldiers even made it to off-limits Monaco, with its casinos and gaming tables.

Lack of money didn't stop the soldiers from having a good time. "Some of us used to sell our cigarettes," said Royce Higa. "Those days, cigarettes went for $20 a carton, as I recall—big money. We had small pay at the time. I don't smoke or drink. My friends liked their beer, so I gave them my beer, but I kept my cigarettes. I went to town and bartered. I heard of guys who sold their coffee, filling the cigarette boxes with used grounds at the bottom and putting about an inch of fresh coffee at the top. They used to sell a lot of bacon grease too. Civilians would scoop up the usable grease with their bread."

As in Italy, wartime poverty in France left powerful impressions on the soldiers. "These are some of the things Americans don't know—that there were people so poor, they would wait all day long for our leftovers and put them in gallon cans," said Higa. "When you looked at that, it was really sad. And women had no chance but to sell themselves. There was prostitution all the time, and people waiting at the dumps for your leftover plates of toast, pile of meat, pancakes."

Consequently, some of the troops didn't eat too much of their food, said Kiyoshi Takasaki. "They just left it ..."

Civilian desperation could also be found in the glitter of Nice, where the women were chic and fashionably dressed. But appearances were deceiving. "This guy from the 100th/442nd who had been in every battle was in a room, pants off, with a woman," said

Public park in Menton. The French Riviera provided a rare respite for men of the 100th/442nd.

John Tsukano. "The door opened and in walked a guy with a gun—her husband. And the husband is a policeman, to top it all. My friend thought, 'I'm going to die.' He was never so scared in his life. He's trying to put his pants on—a very comical scene—when the husband says 'hallo, hallo' and gives him wine. The husband knew what the wife was doing. She had his consent. We in the U.S. can look down on this, but when you're in a (wartime) situation and you need to survive, you'll do virtually anything. Are you going to let your family die?"

THE CHAMPAGNE CAMPAIGN came to an abrupt end in March 1945. Germany was on its last gasp, hurt by a dwindling supply of manpower and gasoline. After the Battle of the Bulge (late 1944), the Allies regained the offensive and pushed into Germany.

Within this historical context, the combat team's 522nd Field Artillery Battalion was sent north to sustain the Seventh Army's final drive into southern Germany. Meanwhile, the main body of the 100th/442nd was assigned in late March 1945 to General Mark Clark's Fifth Army and ordered to crack the German's Gothic Line in Italy, which had withstood repeated Allied assaults.

Shiro Kashino, one of the many remarkable warriors of World War II, was in the stockade during the Champagne Campaign when he got the news about the 442nd's movement to Italy. His journey to the stockade started in England where he was recovering from wounds incurred during the Lost Battalion rescue. Kashino left his hospital bed to rejoin his unit in southern France. "We were in this bar at Sospel when some MPs ordered us to leave. During the fight, their officer in charge got busted up too and we took off. Next morning, about 30 MPs picked us up and put us in jail. We were not

Lizo Honma (fourth from left) and his buddies enjoy Christmas Day 1944 dinner at a private residence in Menton, France. During the Champagne Campaign, some men stayed in a king's mansion, others in large estates, sanitariums or buildings.

released until the very end, when they told us to go and fight during that final push into Italy."

Again, the regiment was called forth to accomplish what major divisions could not do. "Whenever there was a dangerous or desperate situation or a division that couldn't keep up, they'd call for the 442nd and push the guys in there because they knew the young kids were gutsy," said George Goto. "The thing that amazed everybody else so much was that we trusted the man beside us like a brother. You just knew that if the going got real tough, he's going to be there. He's not going to run. He's going to be right beside you. So you had all this confidence. Total confidence. Really, the key was that we trusted each other so much."

From the outset of their wartime tour, the soldiers of the combat team had been a tightly knit group bound by such loyalty. With one exception, when the Antitank Company was temporarily detached from the combat team from July to October 1944 for glider duty, the unit had been inseparable. "I felt badly when we parted from the 522nd because we were so close," said Kashino. "And in the last drive in Italy, when we called for artillery support, there were no effective forward observers. One forward observer, attached to our company in Italy, shot himself in the leg. We were sad our 522nd wasn't with us."

The 522nd left southern France for the new front on March 9, 1945, and blazed a southward path of fast, constant motion through Germany. By March 12, the soldiers were supporting the 63rd Division in Kleinblittersdorf on the east side of the Saar River. "Battery A fired the battalion's first round on German soil at 1135 hours on March 13," declared *High Angle*, the battalion's newspaper. Joseph Hattori, who volunteered for service from a concentration camp at Heart Mountain, was part of A Battery's gun crew.

Until March 21, the 522nd supported the 63rd's attack on the Siegfried Line—Hitler's western life of defense, consisting of concrete roadblocks and tank traps scattered throughout the countryside. From March 21 to March 25, the battalion fired their guns in direct support of the 45th "Thunderbird" Division as it crossed the Rhine River near Worms. "Anytime there was a halfway decent target to shoot at, at least half a dozen artillery units would see the same target at the same time," said Don Shimazu, Headquarters Battery. "The 522nd used to finish the mission before the others got their first rounds out there. Our unit was capable of firing three sets of firing missions simultaneously."

Once the soldiers crossed the Rhine on March 27—they were momentarily attached to the 44th Division at the time—there was no solid resistance. The front was fluid, zigzag, chaotic. "Everything broke loose and we just kept moving fast," said Manabi Hirasaki, C Battery.

Their fast-paced trek through southern Germany became a blur in the minds of the soldiers as they whizzed through numerous towns—from Worms, Mannheim and Heidelburg to Aslen, Dilligen and beyond.

So swift and frenzied was this "rat race" chase, the battalion was sometimes attached to one division in the morning and linked to another that same evening. At other times, the troops found themselves in the unlikely position of being in front of, rather than behind, the infantry. Artillery targets became scarce, and the soldiers could often travel in broad daylight. "The Germans had these highways in 1945—I mean real highways, beautiful, with these cloverleaf intersections," said Kiyoshi Takasaki, C Battery. "We never saw anything like that before in the states or at home. At that time we were moving maybe 50 to 60 miles a day ..."

Within a two-month period, the 522nd answered 52 support calls and served two corps and five divisions, including the 101st Airborne. "We were sort of a rolling battalion," said Francis Tsuzuki, C Battery. "They needed us here—boom boom—they needed us there, and we zoomed ahead. The Germans were retreating so fast. At times we were moving, oh, more than 100 miles a day."

German soldiers fled from towns and villages, protecting not only themselves but also the townspeople, said George Goto. "So we wouldn't blow the towns up, you know. The Germans were fleeing for their lives, yet they wanted to protect the German people they left behind. As soon as the SS moved out, the regular German soldier would quit. The only reason he was fighting was that the SS would have killed him if he didn't. All we could do was try and catch them as they ran out of town."

In one episode, Lieutenant Susumu Ito and Sergeant Fred Y. Oshima were driving through a wooded area, looking for a place to wash their howitzers. Suddenly, the men spotted three German soldiers sitting on the ground just a few yards away. Without firing a single shot, Ito and Oshima seized the three Germans and took them to their C

Battery area. "It was fairly early in the campaign when our particular incident happened," said Ito. "There wasn't much resistance from the Germans, but we weren't expecting to see what we saw."

Later that evening, two scouting parties from C Battery were organized to search for more German troops. Ito and Oshima went in one direction. The other party—Captain William Ratcliffe, 2nd Lieutenant Toru Hirano, Sergeant George Oiye and Tech 4 Yuki Minaga—moved toward a different area. "Hirano and Minaga were off to the flank, while Ratcliffe and I came upon this two-story house, which looked like a hunting lodge," said Oiye. "When we got pretty close to the house, I crawled into a kind of irrigation ditch, looked up and saw this Jerry looking out the window. Simultaneously, I saw a guard standing at the corner of the house. I watched Ratcliffe run straight into him. They frightened each other—I recall Ratcliffe's red handlebar moustache flying up on both sides—but the German threw down his gun. The funniest scene was when the clip fell out Ratcliffe's carbine and he was groping on the ground trying to find it while keeping an eye on his prisoner. That's when I started shooting at the upper window. Ratcliffe also started shooting. The Germans must have thought there were many of us, because they all came out with their hands up. However, the last guy who saw only me started to run and I shot him in the leg. In all, there were more than a dozen prisoners."

Remembered Ratcliffe, "George was an excellent marksman."

Captured prisoners were sent to an assembly area somewhere in the rear, said Royce Higa. "We had to send them back, otherwise we couldn't move with our own unit which was going ahead so fast. We passed through an airfield where jet fighters, tanks and stuff like that were still standing. But nobody was manning them. The captured prisoners I saw had no weapons."

As the 522nd troops advanced, they noticed other signs of the German army's desperation. "We didn't see vehicles, just a lot of horses and wagons," said George Ishihara, B Battery.

There was some resistance, said Hideo Nakamine, B Battery's machine gunner. "We saw a German plane fly over an American military convoy behind our lines and drop anti-personnel bombs. Then it came close by us, flying at treetop height. I remember firing on it. As it flew away, I saw black smoke escaping from the airplane. I know that plane didn't make it."

The men moved so quickly during March and most of April, towns and villages became indistinct images in their minds. "We were going all over," said Walter Inouye, a radio operator with B Battery's forward observer team. "Headquarters people were also ahead. They were the survey teams, the liaisons. Liaisons went with the infantry company. I remember bombed-out buildings, but I don't remember the names of towns. It was hectic and I didn't have much time to sleep, so I sometimes dozed as we were moving along."

The 522nd finds a Messerschmitt ME 262 jet fighter, among the first operational military jets, under camouflage in a forest near a German autobahn that served as a runway. "Their jets went whooosh, buzzed us. We never saw anything like that before."

While the main body of the 522nd proceeded on its southward path, advance scouts like Inouye were scattered and often far ahead of the battalion. "Our radio had a 25-mile range and we'd be out of range of our headquarters. The liaison would then act as a relay between us and headquarters."

During the last week of April 1945, some of the fast-moving soldiers froze in their tracks. They had seen horror throughout the war, but these images were different—ghosts, almost surrealistic spectres of skin and bones with sunken eyes, hollow cheeks and striped suits. They were barely recognizable as human beings. "There was snow and they did not have shoes—their feet were wrapped in burlap," said Inouye. "I understand that the Germans tried to flee with these prisoners (before the Allies arrived), but those who couldn't walk were shot. The live prisoners removed the burlap from the feet of the dead so that they could wear them ... I don't have events in a chronological order, just bits and pieces of images, but I went into a subcamp somewhere. We were downwind of it, and I could smell the stench of something dead. The camp I saw was by a railroad siding, with flatbed cars on the tracks. I thought I was looking at cordwood, but I was staring at cadavers. And somewhere I opened a warehouse and saw hills of shoes, including children's shoes."

Only such items as burlap and striped suits stood between the prisoners and the cold. "We did not have underwear," said Al Lipson, a survivor of Auschwitz, Dachau and several death marches. "And we're marching in the snow with wooden shoes, the snow and ice sticking to them. We didn't stay long at Dachau because I would say April 23 the Germans decided to evacuate some Jews from Dachau."

Lipson, who was forced to labor in a munitions factory until 1944, was one of more than 30,000 registered prisoners at Dachau in 1945. As the Allies were approaching—

Former prisoners with 522nd soldier. "Some were healthy-looking, some were skin and bones. We saw them going through the garbage cans. We gave them rations, cigarettes, that kind of stuff. They were all over the place."

"we knew the Allied Army was coming from France to liberate us"—Lipson somehow survived a harrowing train ride from Dachau to the Tyrol mountains. "Waiting trains were outside the camp—Dachau did not have platforms like Auschwitz, where trains would go inside the train compound. At Dachau, the trains were outside." (The image of his mother, his wife's mother and his 11-year-old sister walking to the gas chamber at Auschwitz remains clear in Lipson's mind. "This never left me.")

Certain memories also remain with George Goto, who encountered some of Dachau's prisoners. "You can't imagine how really pathetic it was to see these people walking with shallow faces, their eyes sunk in. They were just beaten human beings. Actually, everything was gone out of these human beings—they were destroyed and no amount of food or anything like that was going to bring them out of it. It was going to take love and understanding to make them human beings again. But they looked so gruesome. People can't imagine what it was like to see people who were actually nothing but skin and bones. You can't imagine a human being starving other human beings so badly they would get in that condition."

From various sites, soldiers like Inouye and Goto were looking at either the vast death camp known as Dachau or some of its subsidiary camps located in adjacent towns. (There were more than 30 known subcamps.) Dachau, located in the 1,200-year-old Bavarian town of the same name, was the first of such camps established shortly after the Nazis rose to power in 1933.

The main camp itself was a sprawling complex of more than 600 acres—about one square mile. An aerial photo taken in 1945 revealed rows and rows of barracks on one side. Nearby was the crematorium; beyond the crematorium, workshops and garages. The commandant's office was near the center of the complex, a short distance from the camp entrance with its arched doorways. The SS barracks, SS offices, officers' mess hall and officers' quarters were located on the outer fringes of the camp, far from the sights, smells and sounds of the prisoner barracks.

During its 12 years of existence, an estimated 206,000 prisoners and 32,000 deaths were registered at Dachau. However, the actual number of deaths at Dachau, including the victims of death marches, mass extermination and individual executions, will never be known. It is believed there were prisoners from 27 countries interned at Dachau. Shortly before liberation, the SS destroyed many incriminating documents. (Data from *Concentration camp—Dachau, 1933-1945*, International Dachau Committee, Munich, 1978, booklet.)

A declassified U.S. Army document dated May 11, 1990 showed the movement of the 522nd's Headquarters Battery, but not all the details pertaining to troop movements such as Inouye's are listed, said Hideo Nakamine, chairman of the 522nd Dachau Research Committee. (Nakamine was one of the first known individuals to collect data on the 522nd-Dachau connection.) He, like many other 522nd soldiers, reiterated the fact that 522nd scouts were moving so fast at a tumultuous time, it is difficult today to pinpoint with precision the names and locations of the places they encountered at or near Dachau.

In the last week of April 1945, the 522nd was one of many Allied forces approaching the massive camp of Dachau and its numerous subcamps. There are photos, written testimony and eyewitness accounts of the 45th "Thunderbird" Division freeing Dachau, or a portion thereof. Among others known to have been at Dachau—the 42nd Infantry Division. (From the book, *The Liberators*, Simon Weisenthal Center.)

Considering the chaos and the scattered movements of Allied troops, wandering prisoners and fleeing German soldiers that prevailed at the time, it is probable that different units reached camps or portions of camps at various times and locations.

On April 27, 1945, for instance, two days before the official date of Dachau's liberation, the 522nd Headquarters Battery was listed as having been at the town of Horgau, the site of a known Dachau subcamp. On April 28, 1945, the battalion was recorded to be in the vicinity of Bobingen, Germany, near the Dachau subcamp of Augsburg; ("I do remember being at or around Augsburg before April 28, 1945," said Walter Inouye.)

During the last days of April 1945, some 522nd soldiers came upon barracks encircled by barbed wire. The moment was captured for posterity in a diary written by Ichiro Imanura, who belonged to the 522nd's medical detachment. (Imamura died in 1987.) Chester Tanaka, K Company, brought the diary to light in his 1982 book about the 100th/442nd, *Go For Broke*: "Two liaison scouts from the 522nd Field Artillery Battalion, 100th/442nd, were among the first Allied troops to release prisoners in Dachau concentration camp. I watched as one of the scouts used his carbine to shoot off the chain that held the prison gates shut. He said he just had to open the gates when he saw a couple of the 50 or so prisoners sprawled on the snow-covered ground, moving weakly. They weren't dead as he had first thought.

"When the gates swung open, we got our first good look at the prisoners. Many of them were Jews. They were wearing striped prison suits and round caps. It was cold and the snow was two feet deep in some places. There were no German guards. The prisoners struggled to their feet ... They shuffled weakly out of the compound. They were like skeletons—all skin and bones. Outside the compound, there were a couple of dead cows lying on the road. In minutes, the prisoners had cut off strips of meat, roasted them over a small fire and gobbled the food down. They were starving. After they finished eating, they moved down the road and took shelter in a large stable. They insisted on staying the night in the stable and refused to spend another night in Dachau.

"We had been ordered not to give out rations to the Dachau prisoners because the war was still on and such supplies were needed ... but we gave them food, clothing and medical supplies anyway. The officers looked the other way. These prisoners really needed help ... they were sick, starving and dying. I saw one GI throw some orange peelings into a garbage can. One of the prisoners grabbed the peelings, tore them into small pieces and shared them with the others. They hadn't had any fruits or vegetables in months. They had scurvy. Their teeth were falling out.

"We stayed near Dachau for several days and then got orders to move on. During this time, I found some large chalk-like bars, sort of oval-shaped, with numbers stamped on them. I was about to 'liberate' a couple as souvenirs when an MP told me they were the remains of prisoners. I put the bars back."

Another soldier, Joe Obayashi of Headquarters Battery, remembered of his experience, "We drove on a curved road, came upon a perimeter gate, then a prison wall with the door open, and dazed, sunken eyes peered out."

His story was documented by Ben Tamashiro in the July 4, 1986 issue of *The Hawaii Herald*: "In the forward observer group were Joe Obayashi, Captain Charles Feibleman and another enlisted man. In the early morning of April 29, they drove past one of the open gates of Dachau. The captain remarked to Obayashi that the fleeing German guards must have left some of the gates open. 'We must have been one of the first to get there,' said Obayashi, 'because only a couple of prisoners were wandering about by the open gate, seemingly lost. There were no others outside the fenced area.' The group drove on in search of enemy lines, but were recalled by radio. Returning via the same route, they ran into a sea of prisoners who had by then found the open gates and were pouring out of the camp. 'I had noticed some dead horses on the side of the road we earlier passed by. On the return trip, the prisoners were tearing the dead animals apart, eating the meat raw ...'"

Obayashi said he did not recall seeing any other soldiers at the site. "If there had been fighting around the prison, we would have seen dead or wounded Germans, some indication of a fight, but the Germans just took off. It appeared that way. We don't know what camp this was. But I remember the initial setting—the curved road, the prison, the dead horses. I can never forget that."

Obayashi's friend, Neil Nagareda, was with some other scouts when they ran into a "fully-equipped" soldier by the roadside. The fleeing soldier apparently hadn't had the time, thought or inkling to discard his gear. "He was jabbering something I couldn't understand," Nagareda reflected. "I motioned to him, 'Get in the back.' Later, the radio guy and I talked. We thought maybe we should have captured him. But by the time we looked back, he had disappeared into the forest. And as we proceeded, we ran smack into this prison camp. We didn't know it was a prison camp, until we saw these guys in black and white stripes.

"I saw this prisoner who kept looking into an oven. He went around, shook his head and came in the front again as if to say, 'Why couldn't you hang on for another day or so?' He seemed to be looking for somebody ... Before this, I'd seen our dead soldiers, and I thought about that German who had his arm sticking out of the ground during the rescue of the Lost Battalion. I didn't feel too bad then because he was a GI and we're expected to die. But not the civilians, not like the ones at Dachau. That prisoner looked confused and lost. So skinny, too. I thought, 'Why did the Germans have to treat civilians like this?'"

Josef Erbs, a prisoner at Dachau, did not know the name of his rescuer but remembered his unusual appearance. "On April 29, a big Oriental man saved my life," said the Rumanian-born Erbs. "I was 18 years old, 76 pounds at the time, barely alive. He picked me up from the ground, inside the camp. His uniform had an emblem— blue, with a white hand and white torch. He was a young Asian man with the American Army. Never before had I seen an Asian man or a black man ...

"I was in Hungary when Hitler came in 1940. (When captured in May 1944), I was put in Dachau for many months. On that afternoon, this Japanese American came and saved my life. I was on the ground, couldn't walk. I was so out of it. If the war had lasted another day, I would not have lived through it. I was on my last breath. I drank some caraway soup. Up to that time, I felt alone in the whole world."

A United Nations document revealed the extent of his broken heart. Erbs' father, Juda, died at Dachau on December 5, 1944 at the age of 44. Josef, who was deemed able-bodied, was shipped to several subcamps, Kaufering and Landsberg among them, before he was returned to the main one.

"On April 28, 1945, Josef Erbs was taken by train from Kaufering back to the main camp," said a long time friend of Erbs. "The train was strafed by the United States Air Force, so the prisoners were left in the boxcar until the morning of April 29, when the SS unlocked the cars. In the afternoon, American soldiers—darker-skinned, straight

black hair, with different-shaped faces and eyes—arrived at Dachau. The Japanese American soldier carried Erbs to an Army hospital."

Though they may not have realized the full impact at the time, the 522nd soldiers were bearing witness to one of the most disturbing chapters in human history. Soldier after soldier observed the consequences of inhumanity as they traveled in the area of Munich and nearby Dachau. Thousands of displaced persons wandered aimlessly about in their striped rags—souls of skin and bones and deep, sunken eyes.

"Most of them looked half-dead—skinny, skinny," said Kiyoshi Takasaki. "And then the trucks, the MPs, would come and say, 'Don't feed the prisoners,' that they're going to bring soup kitchens or whatever. They figured if we fed them solid food, the prisoners could drop and die. I saw thousands of them. Then I saw a dead cow, all bones, because the prisoners ate everything."

Takasaki and his buddies were traveling in a convoy of trucks when someone remarked, "Oh what a nice place to have lunch." They stopped at the spot to eat their lunches. While eating, Takasaki noticed it was so quiet "you could hear a pin drop. We looked around and there must have been 5,000 prisoners watching us. We were scared because we figured if the prisoners ever stampeded toward us, we were done for. I don't know who, but someone said, 'Let's get out of here, leave your food, don't run.' The prisoners went for the leftover food. They were orderly. Fortunately, nobody panicked. They were probably too weak to do anything. They showed us the bread they were eating—about 90 percent sawdust, 10 percent flour. That, and soup. I would imagine fewer than 500 calories a day. So I think that was a strategy—use them as long as they could on a minimum diet and if they died, they died. Meantime, the laborers built all these roads and highways."

Forward observer Susumu Ito recalled seeing large numbers of people along the road. "Many died there, just lying on the road, with their striped clothes. That's all they had. They were emaciated. Many could hardly walk."

Said Francis Tsuzuki, "Many of us gave them cigarettes or rations. We saw them going through the garbage cans."

George Oiye cannot forget the sight of the prisoners in striped pajamas. "It was a shock. I thought they were POWs, personally. That's a lot different than being an inmate of a concentration camp. These were inmates of an extermination camp. They didn't ask for food, but their eyes did. Even though we were liberating them, it wasn't our job to take care of them. But we did."

Said George Goto, "But the minute you gave them something, they got violently sick. And some dropped over dead. It was too much for their system because they hadn't been eating like that. We had made some potato soup and gave them the soup. Liquid like that. It made them ill, but at least some of it stayed down.

"I remember one person who sat down on the side of the road and just laid over and died. I don't know if he died because he was so happy to get out, or what. But he just sat down on the road, laid down and died."

Many laid down in large numbers and just gave up, said Joseph Hattori. "At dusk, I saw maybe 100 to 150 concentration camp inmates at a small town near Dachau. I know at least 65 of them died overnight from malnutrition. The townspeople told us. The prisoners were just skin and bones, you know."

When George Ishihara reached Dachau, he, too, was startled by the scene before him. "The thing that hit me most … when we were right outside the gates, I saw this horse. It was like a carcass of a horse, right there. I said, 'Holy Moses, look at these guys—they just cleaned that thing up.' All that was left was bones, a skeleton of a horse there. I vividly remember seeing some guys in these striped uniforms, skinny looking guys."

Some of the men came upon something that looked like piles of cordwood, a sight similar to what radio operator Walter Inouye had seen as he traveled with his forward observer party well in advance of the main body of the 522nd. "We came by with our trucks and saw these bleached-out bodies by the furnaces," said George Goto. "The Nazis didn't have time to burn them. They had to leave. You could see the smoke from the furnaces. Anybody (who came upon the bodies) would think they were piles of wood, because they were bleached-out white human bodies. Nothing there, but bleached-out bone."

Appalling scene after appalling scene confronted the soldiers in a seemingly endless stream. Kiyoshi Takasaki entered a compound with a "fairly small" reception area. "I remember there was still blood on the walls. I think they were beaten up there. I recall seeing some dead bodies on the freight train parked right outside on the railroad track. They couldn't make it. I believe they were from Lithuania and Estonia. We didn't know these things existed, then we were told. They took us to all the ovens and stuff right in camp. They showed us the ovens, still warm. They were huge things where you just shoved the body in."

At the main compound —"the command building"—Don Shimazu recalled seeing a known political dissident, the Reverend Martin Niemoeller. He wore the striped garb. "I saw a *haole* GI at the receiving desk, and that's when I saw Martin Niemoeller," said Shimazu. "I recognized him immediately from pictures I had seen of him in my high school social studies class. I was impressed by the air of serenity about him. The GI at the desk was taking care of paperwork."

Some soldiers of the 522nd were elsewhere. Lieutenant James Mizuno, a B Battery forward observer, led his men to free French POWs at one subcamp, exactly where he did not know. Before he died in 1989, Mizuno shared his experience with the 100th's journalist, Ben Tamashiro, in a story published in the May 18, 1990 issue of *The Hawaii Herald Japanese American Journal*. Mizuno, whose family was interned in the U.S. at the time, believed the prison he freed was south of Munich, near Dachau. The troops were

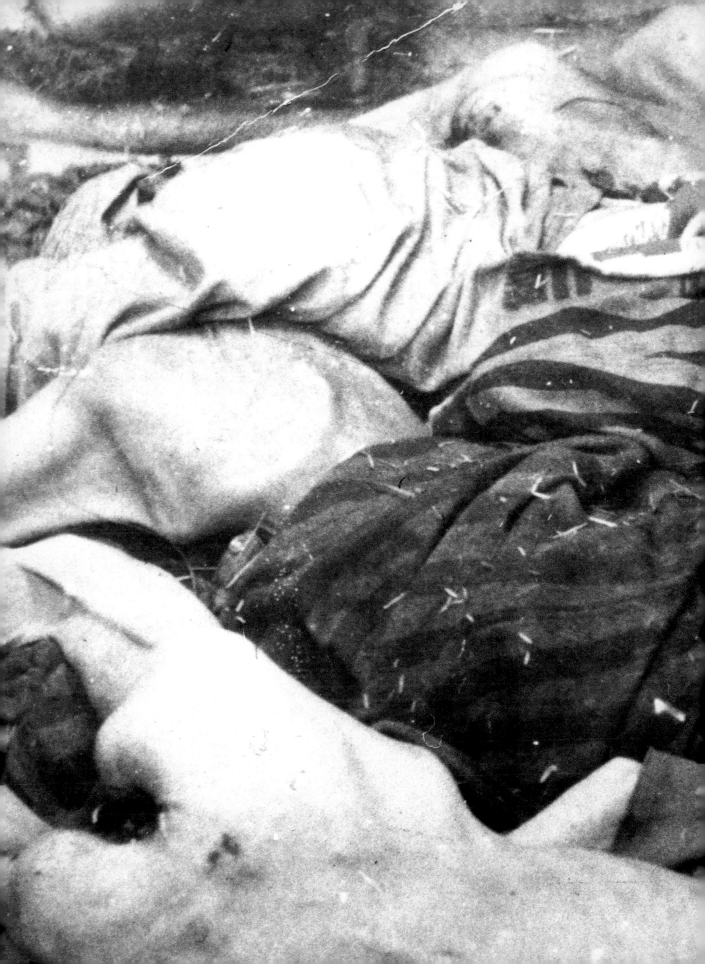

on a small hill, he told Tamashiro.

"Looking down we could see all the prisoners in there. We looked at the towers and there were no guards, so we said, 'Let's take a chance.' I went down to the gate. The majority were French prisoners, not concentration camp people. They were afraid to come out because even though the guards weren't around, they didn't want to take a chance. But they saw our American uniforms, and I told them, 'Come on out.' They said, 'Which way to France?' I pointed, and they all took off."

As liberation was taking place at Dachau's main and subsidiary camps, Hideo Nakamine searched the faces of freed prisoners. "I saw thousands of American troops who had been prisoners wearing American uniforms as our convoy traveled near Munich. We couldn't do so at the time, but I wished we could have stopped and asked the soldiers questions. My cousin, Roy Nakamine, was at a Dachau subcamp."

ROY NAKAMINE SENSED something unusual was happening near his prison, Stalag 7A, on the evening of April 28, 1945. "I think the Germans ran away that night because when I looked the next day, there were no guards around. On April 29, we heard the Allied troops coming—we could hear artillery shells in the distance and we thought, 'Hey, they're close by.' When they passed through, we got some bread to eat—that's the thing that comes to mind. I had tears in my eyes because I was so happy they came."

Stan Akita, located in a different section of Stalag 7A, remembered the moments before and after liberation. "It was about 9 p.m., and since there was no electricity, candles were used," he wrote in his diary. "Most of the men were fast asleep. Suddenly a few of us heard the staccato of an American machine gun. It was definitely not German. We jumped up, aroused the others, but nothing happened. Those who were aroused felt we were hearing things. We went back to sleep. The next day, nothing happened. It made those of us who heard the machine gun look bad. The following night we heard a battle royal taking place in the woods nearby. We could hear the rat-tat-tat of American machine guns and the brrrrrp of a German machine gun. This night, everybody heard it. We lit up all the available candles and packed our meager belongings, prepared to go at a moment's notice. The guards locked the barn …

"Bright and early the next morning, a guard unlocked the doors. We saw only a handful left out of the 50 or so guards. All the buildings in the village had white flags stuck out from their windows. This village of about 50 families was surrounded by a wide meadow. A wooded forest surrounded this meadow. From these woods, we saw American tanks rolling out. We knew that we were liberated. The first thing the tankers offered us was a few loaves of white American bread. After six months of hard brown 'sawdust' bread, this white bread looked, felt and tasted more like cake than anything else."

In still another compound at Stalag 7A, Oscar Miyashiro was unaware of anything extraordinary the night before his liberation. "But in the morning, there were no guards to be found. I saw some American troops around the camp. We saw a tank entering at a distance. I was told, 'That's General Patton.' We stayed at the camp for several days. I remember crawling under the barbed wire to get food from the village … Later, they took us to an airstrip to fly to Le Havre, France (an Allied staging area for troops returning to the U.S.), a camp known as 'Lucky Strike,' from where we were shipped back to the Mainland. Our plane was shot at by Germans, who didn't know the war was practically over."

George Mine, confined for six months at Stalag 3A in Luckenwald, Germany, wondered why the camp guards had disappeared. (Before Stalag 3A, Mine spent four months at Stalag 3B near Frankfurt.) "About a day and a half before the Russians came in, the camp was declared open because the Germans had fled. For security, we placed white sheets on all the fencing, so that any military force who came through would know that we were a neutral zone. Later, the Americans arrived and relieved the Russians."

As soon as he was evacuated from the camp, Mine caught a plane to Le Havre, France, sailed on a troop carrier to New Jersey and took a train to the West Coast. "The train was made up of former prisoners of war who were being dropped off at different points along the way to Fort Bill, California. I ended up by myself, so I had to wait for others who were also heading home to Hawaii. Before I arrived in California, guys from the 100th and 442nd had been shipped home to Hawaii as a contingent. But we unattached individuals had to wait until another group accumulated. While we waited, we sometimes would go to a nearby town. It didn't happen to me, but there were incidents in which racial slurs were made against our Japanese American soldiers, so there were fights."

U. S. ARMY HOSPITAL SHIP "ALGONQUIN" ARRIVES AT PORT OF EMBARKATION CHARLESTON, S. C.

Photo by U. S. Army Signal Corps

Turtle Omiya, Kenneth Otagaki and Walter Matsumoto were among the thousands of wounded soldiers who came home via hospital ships like these.

Occupation

NOT ALL OF THE SOLDIERS of the 100th/442nd reached their Hawaii or Mainland homes at the same time. Many were recuperating from grievous injuries in hospitals far from home; others were part of an occupation force.

Just before the war in Europe officially ended on May 7, 1945, the 522nd was among the U.S. forces at Berchtesgaden, Germany, where it was believed Hitler would make a last stand. At about that time, 522nd soldier Harold Ueoka was in a French hospital, recovering from a severe outbreak of dermatitis on his hand. He had been hospitalized during the 522nd's rapid drive through southern Germany. "On May 8, I was going from the hospital to the train to join my unit when I saw the headline on the *Stars and Stripes* newspaper—'War is Over.' I had chicken skin."

Ueoka joined his battalion at the German town of Donauworth, on the banks of the Danube River, where the 522nd was to spend the next six months as an occupation force. There, in and around Donauworth, postwar duties exposed the soldiers to a variety of experiences. From that station, for instance, Ueoka was able to travel and see what others before him had witnessed at Dachau.

"(At Dachau), we went into a building which was very dark inside, and went down to the cellar," he reflected. "We went slowly down because we didn't know where the end was. Then our footing got wavy, and we wondered, 'What was that?' Someone said, 'Those are urns all piled up.' Dachau was on our way to Munich and Berchtesgaden, where we visited the homes of Hitler, the SS and Herman Goering. They were bombed out. I have a picture taken from the second floor of Hitler's house, with a beautiful view of the countryside."

One of the 522nd's occupation duties was to gather displaced persons, including Jews, into a central area and return them to their home countries. "But where could we send the Jews?" said Walter Inouye. "This rounding up was happening before Israel was established. The Jews were traveling in ships all over the place like boat people."

Prisoners from Dachau told Inouye something that confirmed the suspicions of soldiers like Neil Nagareda, who expressed that there were invisible heroes at the Lost Battalion rescue in France and elsewhere in Europe. During that campaign, Nagareda had come across several shells that turned out to be "duds." While some shells may indeed have been accidentally flawed, the number of duds the soldiers encountered was too high to be sheer coincidence, said Nagareda.

Inouye confirmed the suspicion. "We gave the Jewish prisoners from Dachau our rations and cigarettes and we'd talk story. So I heard these displaced people say conscripted workers took their lives in their hands, but they'd sabotage these shells. In my own early experience with a dud, I heard sand was found in it. I believe it. The prisoners felt they had nothing to lose."

One day when Inouye was at Mertingen, near Donauworth, he received another order: "Round up the Russians." He rose at four the next morning to pick up the 100 or so Russians believed to be in the area. "Before we started, people knew we would be picking up Russians. But we couldn't find a single one. About three days later, they started to appear again."

Nearby, a farmer was having trouble with some displaced people who shot at him as they foraged for food and water. Inouye was assigned to protect the farmer. "His name was Linke, and he was a Russian who had escaped his country during the Bolshevik Revolution in 1917," said Inouye. "The farmer employed tenant farmers—sharecroppers."

Inouye saw one sharecropper who looked all too familiar. "I recognized Dachau prisoners. This one was about 24, but his eyes were sunken, his teeth were almost gone, his hair was gray and he still suffered from malnutrition. His joints at the wrists and elbows were large, with very little meat in between. It was just hanging there. He was one of the prisoners we were supposed to have rounded up and returned to south Russia, lower (Soviet) Georgia."

Inouye was able to understand the prisoner's situation better when he spoke to the farmer's wife, who understood English. "I asked her, 'Why doesn't he want to go home?' She said, 'He knows he's an alien in a foreign country, but he believes as long as he works, he'll get three meals a day, a roof over his head, and, most important, he'll be able to see the sun.' It dawned on me a few years later, what the prisoner was trying to tell me. This Russian man had taken some of the worst punishment a human could take. Yet, he felt it better for him to stay there than return to Russia."

Inouye mentally connected the sharecropper episode with an earlier incident, when he had been on a reconnaisance mission during the 522nd's swift advance through southern Germany. He was with a patrol, walking ahead of the infantry, when the men came to a town and looked around for a place to sleep. "Suddenly, German soldiers came around, about 150 men, wanting to surrender. This was not the SS or the Wehrmacht,

(Left) Francis Tsuzuki at Donauworth, Germany. (Right) "Mr. Blum," a displaced person, and Royce Higa. Germany, 1945.

the regular German Army. This was more like the home guard. I didn't know what to do with them. The others were way behind us. I said, 'Leave your weapons here.' This German asked, 'Will you allow us to keep our weapons?' I said, 'Why?' He said, 'We'll help you fight the Russian (Communists).' Now I know why. I couldn't report these things at that time. It was confusing. I didn't know what was going on politically. It didn't dawn on me until I returned to Hawaii."

Like Inouye, other 522nd troops on occupation duty in Germany were doing what they could to help displaced people. Royce Higa and John Ogashima, A Battery, were assigned to assist a "Mr. Blum," a Lithuanian refugee, in finding his wife and two sons. "I don't know how we were selected, but we didn't question it," said Higa. "In fact, I was very excited about the assignment."

The men loaded their jeep and a trailer with gasoline, food and supplies. "And together we went, from Donauworth, Augsberg, Munich, Berchtesgaden, Salzburg and into the woods to mountains somewhere in Austria. And everyplace we'd go, he'd ask people if they saw any camp for displaced persons."

Higa and his party traveled on a narrow road to a British sector in the mountains. The British told them there were no camps for displaced people in the area and sent the men down the mountain. That evening, they stayed at a village guest house where beer was served. Some people peered at the men behind the safety of a curtain, saying, "Russky, Russky."

"According to the owner, the people there were afraid of John and me," said Higa. "They thought we were Russians. Apparently, they had not seen any Japanese before."

There, the men learned of a refugee camp in Linz, Austria, and immediately headed for the site, asking for directions along the way. "We went into this camp and found his wife," said Higa.

While the overjoyed Lithuanian was talking to his wife inside the compound, Higa and Ogashima were not able to witness the momentous occasion or celebrate the success of their mission. "American guns were pointed at us—50-calibre guns from a halftrack (combination truck and tank)," remembered Higa. "They demanded our credentials. They thought we were black marketeers because we were loaded with gasoline, food and all kinds. Hey, people don't realize that some American GIs used to steal and sell things by the truckloads—cigarettes, gasoline, tires, so on. But they let us go after we explained our mission. This experience scared the hell out of us. "

Higa and Ogashima took the reunited pair back to Donauworth, where the couple found an apartment. "I still recall the celebration dinner at their home—tomato salad, potato onion soup and C rations," said Higa. "Food didn't matter. Just seeing them together was tremendous. Through the excitement, we failed to ask Blum about their sons. I don't know what happened to the children. But I got the impression that they had not survived."

Beyond the Po

DURING THE 552ND'S FAST DRIVE through southern Germany in April 1945, its "mother" outfit, the 442nd, had been involved in action of its own.

At the request of General Mark Clark the main body of 442nd soldiers was sent to Italy under secrecy to do what no other division was able to do: spearhead an assault on the western sector of the Gothic Line—rock and concrete fortifications high in the rugged Apennines of northern Italy, where Germans had been entrenched for several months. Steep cliffs, an estimated 3,000 feet high, stood between the Germans' backs and the Japanese American soldiers. Any ascent, any sound, could leave the men vulnerable to machine gun fire from above and wipe them out. Even if they succeeded in the "back door attack," the soldiers still faced hills and chains of hills held by heavily fortified Germans. Retrospectively, the campaign's strategies, including diversionary tactics, were brilliant.

With full battle gear on their backs, the soldiers climbed the cliffs in darkness on April 5, 1945. "Even billy goats refuse to climb it," remarked one soldier.

"I remember the night we walked up with an Italian guide who took us to the steep back of the mountains," said Shiro Kashino. "And it was sheer cliff. All of the 442nd— the 100th, 2nd and 3rd battalions—moved up the cliffs. It's hard to believe, but the men did this by climbing hand-to-hand, hanging onto rocks and shrubs. We started at night. By early morning we reached the top of that cliff. We got up behind them, then started the attack. I think the surprise element got them. I don't think the Germans expected us up there. They'd been sitting there for five months. I wondered why Americans hadn't tried this cliff climb before. On the way to the top, I know some of our guys fell. I could hear helmets falling off and rocks rolling down. But no one cried out."

Kashino received another of his numerous battle injuries during the troops' drive through hills and valleys. He was near a town, when an artillery shell hit the corner of a building. The impact hurled a large piece of brick on Kashino's head, throwing him backwards. "Luckily, I had my helmet on, (but) I was bleeding from the nose and mouth."

Before Kashino went to an aid station, he gave his tommy gun, binoculars and wrist watch to Tadao Hayashi and said, "You take over."

Kashino and the California-born Hayashi were buddies. Before they left France for this last battle in Italy, the men and some other 442nd soldiers were imprisoned in a stockade because of a bar brawl during the Champagne Campaign. Hayashi, Kashino and their other cellmates were released from their stockade to fight in the 442nd's final campaign. "When I was at the aid station, I heard Hayashi was missing in action," said

Kashino. "So I took off to the front line again, but they found his body. We were close. It was a tragedy that he had spent his (Champagne Campaign) time in the stockade."

When their fighting in Italy was over, the 442nd's soldiers had suffered more losses: 56 killed and 247 wounded. The combat team was honored with its seventh Presidential Unit Citation, the 2nd Battalion received a special Unit Citation for its exploits in the area of Massa, Italy, and the 100th's PFC Sadao S. Munemori of Los Angeles became the first Japanese American soldier to receive a Congressional Medal of Honor, posthumously. He leaped upon a grenade, covering it with his body so that the explosion would not endanger his friends.

Kashino and others were assigned to guard German prisoners when the war in Italy ended on May 2, 1945. He sat in a guard tower which overlooked the prisoner compound. "And it reminded us of our concentration camp back home in Minidoka, Idaho. The layout was square. In the middle was a mess hall, bath and shower room, the barracks."

After Kashino finished his Italian tour, he still faced a court martial for his part in the bar brawl. "I remember this Captain Wheatley—he took over when Captain Byrne was killed at the Lost Battalion rescue—who said, 'If you guys live through this war, I guarantee you guys won't ever have to take a court martial.' But he was killed."

Kashino was found guilty "right away" and served 77 days behind the barbed wires of the regiment's stockade.

AT WAR'S END, the casualty list of the 100th/442nd was swollen with the dead and wounded. Some of the injured were seriously hurt, and they spent long months in military hospitals in France, England and Italy. Lieutenant Daniel K. Inouye, E Company, 2nd Battalion, and Lieutenant Walter Matsumoto, 232nd Combat Engineer Company, were wounded during their final campaign in Italy.

"Dan and I were together at a general hospital in Leghorn, Italy," said Matsumoto, who lost his left eye, the hearing in his right ear and the nerves of his right arm. "Dan used to push me around in my wheelchair since shrapnel also pierced my shoe and broke two bones in my right foot. Dan lost his arm, but he was able to walk around. We were at Leghorn for about 45 days."

When Matsumoto regained some strength, he and other wounded soldiers were shipped to the U.S. via a circuitous route—from Naples to Oran to Casablanca to the Azores to Miami. "From Miami, I flew to Valley Forge, Pennsylvania, because of its eye hospital," said Matsumoto. "I was there for 10 months."

Tadao Beppu, M Company, 3rd Battalion, was recuperating at a hospital in England. His shin bone had been shattered during the Lost Battalion rescue in October 1944. "I spent about three months in a Paris hospital, then was moved to a hospital in England for another six months. "I couldn't walk, but they didn't have enough wheelchairs and crutches in the hospital."

The 100th's Kenneth Otagaki had been at Walter Reed Army Hospital, recovering from severe injuries incurred in Italy in early 1944. He lost his right leg at the hip, his right eye, two fingers from his right hand and a large chunk of his chest. For a while it seemed Otagaki would not make it. "He was comatose," said Albert Oki, his buddy.

"In those days, there wasn't enough penicillin to go around so wounds got infected and sapped your energy," said Otagaki. "Doctors said, 'There's no hope for this guy.' A priest came by and said, 'Your records show you are an aetheist. In order to have peaceful rest, can I get you into a religion.' I said, 'I don't care.' So he baptized me a Catholic. Can you imagine that? He said, 'Doesn't matter, this just makes it formal.'

"I was almost dead when they decided to give me the penicillin. Like a miracle, it turned me around. I used to weigh so little in those days, the nurses would carry me when they changed the bedding. In a joking way, I hung on to this big-breasted nurse and she said, 'You must be getting well.'"

K Company's Joe Shimamura doing six months "duty" at Halloran General Hospital in Staten Island, New York, 1945. Suffering from trench feet and an injured shoulder that needed surgery, Shimamura returned home aboard the hospital ship, U.S.S. Frances Y. Slanger.

Moment of reflection in the resort area of Koenigsee in postwar Germany.

(Upper left) Lady love. Maritime Alps, Winter 1944-45. (Upper right) "Kuncho" Maruo,
with a flower lei made by Antitank Company men in Monaco. Winter 1944-45.
(Lower left) Roy Okubo, Nice, France. Winter 1945. (Lower right) "Mutt" Kobashigawa,
B Battery, 522nd Field Artillery Battalion. Germany, 1945.

(Upper left) Robert "Pop" Takemura, Antitank Company in Menton. Winter 1944-45. (Upper right) "Once around the park, please." Iizo Honma in Nice, France. Winter 1944-45. (Lower left) Shigeru Tomita, 100th Battalion. (Lower right) Hideo Nakamine of the 522nd's B Battery in Menton, France. Winter 1944-45.

When a grieving mother requested a picture of her son's grave in Italy, several soldiers of the 442nd's F Company spent their 3-day pass driving hundreds of miles to honor her wish. (L-R), Sadao Okuhara, Mamoru Hiranaka, Yoshio Yamamoto, Masatoshi Hokama and Katsuji Nakamura.

Epilogue

WHEN THE UNITED STATES dropped its atomic bombs on Hiroshima and Nagasaki in August 1945, the war in the Pacific was over. War's end, however, did not necessarily mean peace. For many of the soldiers who served with the 100th/442nd, the MIS and the 1399 Engineer Construction Battalion, different battles were just beginning—at home and afar.

Japanese American soldiers serving with the U.S. Army's Military Intelligence Service (MIS), for instance, converged in Japan during American occupation and rendered valuable aid to a devastated people. Would Asian faces in American uniforms perplex the Japanese? wondered many of the men. "We were afraid we would be stoned by the Japanese—traitor and all that," said Kiyoshi Yoshimura, who spent part of his MIS tour in Australia with the Allied Translator and Interpreter Service (ATIS).

Compassion and understanding prevailed, however, as the soldiers helped civilians in a city devastated by bombs. "The trains that went out from Tokyo to the countryside (for food) were all stacked with people—on top, hanging out the sides," said Hakobu Kumagai, an MIS radio interceptor in New Guinea and the Philippines.

Arthur Komori, a valuable intelligence aide with General MacArthur's staff since spring 1941, helped starving families by sharing his K rations and cigarettes. "They really hungered for cigarettes," he recalled. "Tokyo was all flattened, and people were living in holes with corrugated roofs. They were desperate for food. I remember a Japanese man who wanted me to exchange his wife's silk clothing for a warm burberry overcoat. It was so cold. So we placed an ad in a Japanese American paper. A major general had a tan burberry coat so I went along to help make the exchange."

To the disappointment of many Japanese American veterans, compassion and understanding were often harder to find at home in the United States. The blood spilled by them—indeed, the proportionately large number of wartime casualties suffered by all ethnic minorities in America—seemed to have little effect on the status quo. Anti-Japanese sentiment was especially strong on the West Coast, where soldiers' homes were shot at, vandalized, looted or burned. Restaurants and barbershops made it known that they didn't serve "Japs." One returning soldier, a survivor of the Rescue of the Lost Battalion, was welcomed by a storefront sign—"No Japs Wanted."

George Oiye returned to Montana after his honorable discharge in 1946. "I went back to school and had a nervous breakdown. Also, my ears were so badly damaged in the war that they rang—they still ring—louder than any noise you can make. It was hard to adjust at first—one ear rings at a different frequency than the other, so sometimes they go out of whack. It took a long time to rehabilitate. I worked on the railroad for a year, just to get away from people and other pressures. Then I got into aerospace and laser engineering."

At a time when maintaining a "proper" image was foremost, especially in Asian cultures, many soldiers had to deny or hide their feelings, said Yuki Minaga. "I used to have nightmares, and was beating the walls. We were lectured about not breaking down. But I almost had a breakdown."

Upon his return to the U.S., Shiro Kashino married a lovely woman he met while he was interned at Minidoka, Idaho. Filled with hope for the future, the newlyweds looked for a house of their own. "But we were told by the real estate broker, 'We're saving our homes for returning veterans,'" said Kashino's wife, Louise. "And Kash said, 'What do you think I am?' and chased the guy around the office."

Discrimination followed Kashino when he tried to get into the trade unions. "I tried to get a job and they said, 'We're saving our jobs for returning vets.' In 1954, I got into the Teamsters union, auto sales, because I finally got a job. Funny thing, there weren't other *niseis* around. So when there was a strike five months long, I picketed every day for those five months. Then the union wanted more Japanese Americans ... At home we kept our yards clean, were good neighbors. Once we got in—whether it was a home, union, job, whatever—it wasn't so bad, but we had so many fights back then. Why did we have to prove ourselves over and over?"

Like many other returning veterans, Kashino suffered from ear problems. When he went to get his ears checked, the doctor queried and lectured the veteran: "Are you Buddhist? Do you believe in God? You'd better pray that your ears will get better because there's nothing I can do for you."

Not wanting to openly complain about his ear injury—Kashino viewed his physical disabilities as minor, when compared to what he witnessed during the war—he did nothing about the hardship for 35 years. Kashino did not report the problem to the Veterans Administration. He did not request compensation. "He figured he came home alive, while others did not," said Louise. "But 35 years later, he finally got fitted for a hearing aid."

Unfortunately, one year before the VA reviewed Kashino's case, a newly passed law allowed retroactive compensation only to the date of the law. If Kashino had applied for his benefits earlier, he would have been eligible for pay retroactive to the time of injury.

In Oregon, sixteen names of Japanese American soldiers were removed from a county's war memorial by members of the Hood River American Legion Post. This occurred in December 1944, shortly after the 100th/442nd's agonizing experiences in France's Vosges mountains. Among the names removed: Frank Hachiya, an MIS soldier who was posthumously awarded the Distinguished Service Cross for gallantry in action during his secret service in the Pacific.

Lynn Crost, war correspondent and friend of the 100th/442nd, expressed her concerns in a June 17, 1945 letter to Harold Ickes, Secretary of the Interior. She wrote in part about Seiji Nishioka, a soldier she had met a few weeks earlier while visiting wounded men in general hospitals in Naples, Italy. Nishioka was a soldier whose name was among those removed from the Hood River memorial. "He was evidently in such pain that I did not talk much to him that day, but (I) returned later ... I remarked about the change in his appearance and he replied, 'They just gave me another blood transfusion.' He couldn't quite remember whether it had been the 14th or 15th such transfusion. He had had five operations, including some on his stomach where shrapnel had penetrated from his back ...

"He is 24 years old. He has been the main support of his family since he was 14— when his father died. His mother, sister and a brother, 16, are at a relocation camp in Wyoming. He had to lease his farm in Hood River when he was evacuated. He doesn't know whether to return because of the racial situation there. And, if he does return, he doesn't know whether his legs will ever be strong enough to permit him to work his farm again. He was wounded in a foxhole in Carrara, during the final push up the west coast of Italy."

Strong protests against the Hood River action from people overseas and around the nation resulted in a reluctant restoration of the names to the memorial. The extraordinary combat record of the Japanese Americans did little to sway the legionaires' minds. Some had argued that the soldiers' achievements in Europe could be discounted since the Japanese "enjoyed fighting against white men." Others, obviously ignoring the work of the Japanese American MIS in the Pacific, charged that the soldiers' loyalty really belonged to the Emperor of Japan.

Japanese American soldiers were victims of societal ignorance and stereotype no matter which way they turned. In the same letter to U.S. Secretary of the Interior Harold Ickes (about a month and a half before the end of the war in the Pacific), Crost wrote: "Regarding the recently reported War Department program of using *nisei* troops in Japanese uniforms for training GIs for Pacific combat, nothing I can say could convey to you the feeling of consternation it has aroused in 442nd men. Again, I have talked with numerous men of that unit, including some of their Caucasian officers. Their reactions are these ...

"Many have told me they would rather go back into combat anywhere, rather than dress up in Japanese uniforms and use Japanese weapons in this training program. They said they could not understand why Caucasian soldiers could not do the same training inasmuch as *nisei* don't know anything about Japanese warfare in the first place and therefore have to be trained by the War Department in such methods. They believe the use of *nisei* for such work—particularly when they are required to copy Japanese enemy troops to the exact detail of even dress—will serve only to increase racial

Robert Sasaki, L Company, 3rd Battalion, worked for the federal government and later for the 442nd Veterans Club.

antagonism. They think a feeling of doubt and hatred toward Japanese Americans cannot help but be engendered among unthinking GIs who train under such a program."

HAWAII'S RETURNING SOLDIERS had to deal with their own share of conflicts, some of which were fought by making use of the educational benefits offered by the GI Bill of Rights. With their relatively large numbers in the islands, the men pulled together. "I was lucky enough to become an attorney and work on disability cases," said the 100th's Albert Oki, who served for 20 years as a lawyer with the Veterans Administration. "On a percentage basis, our boys took it (the pain). They needed a third party to work with the VA. See, many of their physical injuries were so grossly underrated. There was discrimination there, too. The rate adjudication department was made up mostly of Mainlanders—white people. Their philosophy was, 'We don't have to help these guys too much. They can survive on poi, rice, fish.' The record of the 100th/442nd didn't mean a darn thing to some of the *haoles*."

Oki had a field day representing the veterans. "These poor guys were getting a low rating for their multiple injuries. Take Kanchi Heyada, for instance. He was given an 80 percent rating, but he had practically two legs off. The laws provide special consideration for them, not only 80 percent. He was supposed to be in a higher bracket. But at first they didn't get these things. The (bureaucracy) said, 'We're not going to give the men all of that.' Fortunately, I was able to represent them … and I really enjoyed my work."

One of the disabled veterans was the 100th's Yoshinao "Turtle" Omiya, who had been blinded by shrapnel during action in Italy. During Omiya's recuperation at Valley Forge Hospital in Pennsylvania, Earl Finch of Mississippi, a friend of the 100th/442nd, heard about the veteran's plight. Finch got the Army to send the veteran to Morristown, New Jersey to acquire a seeing-eye dog, Audrey. Upon his return to Hawaii in 1945, Omiya struggled to adapt to his permanent darkness with the reassuring presence of Audrey, the German Shepherd who was his constant companion and joy in life until her death in 1948 when she was accidentally hit by a car. (Omiya's mother and sister cared for him for more than 35 years. Omiya, who never married, died in 1984.)

The veterans needed such friends as Oki and Finch. Little in Hawaii's power structure had changed since the men left the islands' shores barely three years before. Plantation paternalism, job discrimination and social inequities were prevalent.

While Hideo Nakamine had been training at Camp Shelby, Mississippi, his younger brother died from the bubonic plague on the Big Island. The plantation manager displayed no sympathy for the family's loss. "When the manager learned I wasn't working on the plantation any more, that I was in the service, he called another younger brother of mine into the office and told him, 'Your family has to move out within 30 days.' That was the only housing my family had."

Nakamine's grieving family moved to Hilo to live with his married sister in a small, crowded house. "Then they moved to Honolulu and stayed with another brother. My family didn't tell me about this for a long time. My sister, who used to write to me while I was away, never mentioned to me that the family had been kicked out from the plantation."

When Tadao Beppu returned from the war, he noticed that non*haoles* who traveled from Hawaii to the Mainland were still required to show proof of U.S. citizenship. Said Beppu: "This *haole* guy was trying to form a veterans committee right after the war, so we asked, 'Why the hell they do this to us?' He didn't believe us. But one day he passed that immigration station at Ala Moana and saw a Chinese soldier, a captain in the U.S. Army, standing in line with his wife and baby. So he said to me, 'You know I had tears in my eyes when I saw that.' He went to see an official of the steamship company and inquired, 'Why do you do that?' The official told him, 'To protect our flanks because we can be fined for transporting aliens.' The steamship carrier tried to defend its actions.

Tadao Beppu, M Company, 3rd Battalion, rose to political prominence in postwar Hawaii.

Hideo Nakamine, B Battery, 522nd, was employed by the Army as a maintenance electrician after the war.

The whole thing was sickening."

Similarly, Asians were often denied passage on Hawaiian Airlines during the war. Until 1946, the airline employed no Asians as pilots or stewardesses. That year, Asian businessmen, most notably Rudy Tongg, organized Trans-Pacific Airlines, the forerunner of Aloha Airlines. At about that time, Harold Yokoyama started the frustrating process of obtaining some compensation for the loss of his family's fishing boat on the morning of December 8. He got nowhere.

"Why the hell they do that to us?" was just one of the questions the men asked after the war. Soldiers of virtually every ethnic group had lost their lives during the war.

THE IMPACT OF THE WARTIME RECORD of the 100th/442nd could be felt with each passing decade. Especially in Hawaii.

Veterans of the 100th/442nd became Hawaii's many movers and shakers during the vast, complex changes of the postwar era. They and thousands of other Japanese Americans entered the Democratic Party, which wrested control of the territorial legislature from the mainly *haole* Republican Party in November 1954. "The political revolution came from many factors—the Japanese Americans, the strength of unions, an expanding economy and the opening up of Hawaii during World War II," said Franklin Odo, Professor of Ethnic Studies, the University of Hawaii at Manoa. "The war was ironically beneficial in this regard. The power of the Big Five began to wane." (The Big Five referred to corporations—Castle & Cooke, C. Brewer, American Factors, Theo H. Davies, Alexander and Baldwin—controlled by prominent *haole* families with longtime plantation and missionary roots in the islands.)

The era's rising political figures included many veterans of the 100th/442nd—from Masayuki "Spark" Matsunaga of the 100th Infantry Battalion to Daniel K. Inouye of the 442nd Regimental Combat Team. Inouye became the first American of Japanese ancestry to serve in the U.S. Congress when he was elected Hawaii's representative in 1959. Hawaii's voters sent Inouye to the U.S. Senate in 1962, where he continues to work today. Matsunaga served in the U.S Senate from 1976 until his death in 1990.

Hawaii's representation in Congress came after 1959, the year the U.S. territory became a state. The record of the 100th/442nd played an important role in the granting of statehood. "When the 100th was fighting in Italy, we fought with several outfits from the midwest, including the 34th Division, and these *haole* soldiers wrote to their friends and relatives about the Japanese American soldiers," said the 100th's Young Oak Kim. "Word spread, grass roots support grew."

The Lost Battalion rescue in particular had an effect on key members of Congress, explained Hideo Nakamine. "The U.S. Senate and the U.S. House were led by two powerful Texans at the time—Lyndon Johnson and Sam Rayburn."

Wartime sacrifices of the 100th/442nd also contributed to the recognition and redress of a grave wrong—the internment of Japanese Americans during the war. In October 1990, about two years after President Ronald Reagan signed the Civil Liberties Act of 1988 into law, letters of apology and checks for $20,000 each were given to 15,000 of the eldest surviving victims of wartime racism and hysteria. Money, however, was never the issue. "What do you pay a man who lost his mother because she could not stand life in an internment camp any longer and committed suicide?" asked Senator Inouye. "How do you pay a child who saw his father shot because he demonstrated? Three

Lizo Honma, Antitank Company, went to college in Chicago and later worked for Hawaii's criminal justice system.

Royce Higa, A Battery, 522nd, made his mark in public health and social work.

days of indignity is just as bad as three years of it. When Congress passed it (reparations), this was a proud moment for America. Because it takes a big country to admit wrong. There are not many countries that would do this."

KEY TO MAKING REDRESS a reality was the presence and efforts of highly regarded Japanese Americans in the U.S. Congress—Senators Daniel K. Inouye and Spark Matsunaga from Hawaii and Representatives Robert Matsui and Norman Mineta from California. A commission was established to hold hearings and generate interest—it was important that the nation be exposed to the subject.

When the redress hearings reached Seattle in 1980, Louise Kashino attended every session. She was only 15 when her family was suddenly uprooted and interned at Minidoka, Idaho. "My daughters in high school started hearing about this and said, 'What's wrong with you guys? Why didn't you stand up for your rights?' I told them they didn't understand how it was because of the times … I told my kids, 'If we thought about it all the time, we'd be in a loony cage, because you could go crazy thinking about it.'" During the hearings, the Kashinos heard the testimony of a retired general who defended the internment as "military necessity." "The general made the comment, 'A Jap's a Jap,'" said Shiro Kashino of a phrase uttered 40 years before by General John DeWitt.

Many individuals and groups worked hard toward the goal of reparations, including the Japanese American Citizens League, and the National Coalition for Japanese American Redress. "In California, some of the staunchest supporters of reparations were Chinese Americans," said Clifford Uyeda, president of the National Japanese

American Historical Society (NJAHS). "They did not get a penny out of it, but they worked hard. Also the Filipino Americans and many more."

Numerous others, visible and invisible, became actively involved in the passage of the redress bill. Recalled a Korean War veteran and behind-the-scenes worker: "Everything seemed to fall into place. The Speaker of the House was Texan Jim Wright, who had a relative in the Lost Battalion. The subcommittee chairman (of the Judiciary Committee) who handled the redress was Congressman Barney Frank, a Jewish man. We made sure he got the Dachau story. Senator Simpson of Wyoming, a conservative, had belonged to a Boy Scout troop as a teen ager in Wyoming. Congressman Norm Mineta was one of the (interned) who belonged to the troop in the camp. He and Simpson became boyhood friends and continued the friendship. Senator Matsunaga was a friend of Senator Howard Baker, even if they were on opposite sides of the aisle. We were afraid of a presidential veto. Baker had become White House Chief of Staff. Sparky reminded Baker of an incident where a young captain had been sent from the Sixth Army headquarters to intercede in a town which did not want a deceased 442nd soldier buried in its cemetery. And this young captain said, 'American blood that soaks into battle fields is one color—red.' That captain was Ronald Wilson Reagan, and when he signed the bill, the gipper scored a touchdown and won one on his own."

It is possible the redress bill might have emerged sooner if the Dachau story had become widely known years ago, said Hideo Nakamine, chairman of the 522nd Dachau Research Committee of the 100th/442nd. "The Jewish community as well as many others could have been a powerful, vocal force, and a great wrong could have been recognized much earlier. So many internees and veterans have already died."

Susumu Ito, C Battery, 522nd, became a renowned professor at Harvard Medical School.

Walter Inouye, B Battery, 522nd, put his mechanical talents to work as an appliance service manager.

Hideo Nakamine's work in preserving the history of the combat team's 522nd Field Artillery Battalion and its role at Dachau has been a longstanding one. "After we came home from the war, I started to read books and watch television programs about the Jewish people and it hit me, 'Hey, we were at Dachau.' Then, Chester Tanaka documented the diary of Ichiro Imamura in his book, *Go For Broke*."

Call it fate, coincidence, whatever, but that all-important diary was obtained because Tanaka happened to be at right place at the right time—filling the gas tank of his car at a San Francisco service station in late 1981. "A car pulled up behind me and the driver, a Japanese American who worked for the state, noticed the frame of my license plate which said, 'Go For Broke—100th/442nd,'" recalled Tanaka. He gave me his card and said his relative with the 522nd had opened a gate at Dachau concentration camp. My hair stood up. I didn't believe it at first …"

One event led to another and Tanaka eventually ended up talking to Ichiro Imamura. "I saw his notes in an album. He was dying of cancer at that time. I called Eric Saul (then the curator of the Presidio Army Museum in San Francisco) and my friend, Tom Kawaguchi, and asked, 'Have you heard of this?' Both said, 'No.' I wrote the story up and we stopped the presses for six months on the *Go For Broke* book. I did more checking. Another friend, Dick Hayashi, said, 'Check it out with Susumu Ito.' I called a number in Massachusetts and got a Professor Ito at Harvard Medical School. To my surprise, he had hundreds of photographs and many rolls of negatives still undeveloped. Amazingly, they were in good shape. I found out later that the 522nd soldiers had (confiscated) a German photo lab on wheels during their journey. He sent us the pictures and there were the photos of Dachau and the prisoners. Things started to come together.

Joe Shimamura, K Company, 3rd Battalion, went to school in Chicago and became a successful optometrist.

Then I heard some people mention that they had seen Japanese American POWs. The story tightened up even more."

There are pieces to the puzzle that may never be found. It is believed that one of the scouts mentioned in Imamura's diary was Shozo Kajioka. ("I watched as one of the scouts used his carbine to shoot off the chain that held the prison gate shut," wrote Imamura.) During his lifetime, several people, recognizing the historical significance of the event, asked the former scout about his Dachau experience. "He didn't want to talk," said Nakamine.

In 1984, as in previous years, some 100th/442nd veterans returned to Bruyeres, France, to honor the memory of the soldiers who were killed in one terrible month of battle. About 15 members of the 522nd made a side trip to Dachau, the first group of the battalion to return to the site.

Although some information about the 522nd's presence at Dachau was known publicly by the mid-1980s, much of the international response was sparked by Ben Tamashiro's 1986 article in *The Hawaii Herald*, "The Liberation of Dachau." Since then, educators, writers and filmmakers, including film crews from Japan, have recorded the 522nd's experience.

Many of them received their help from Nakamine, who spent a considerable amount of time, energy and personal funds to preserve the history of the 522nd's encounter at Dachau. Through the years of researching and collecting data, Nakamine has donated numerous photographs, documents and maps to such groups and institutions as the Bishop Museum, the Center for Holocaust Studies, the 100th/442nd Historical Committee and the Go For Broke National Veterans Association. His efforts have not gone unappreciated. The State of Hawaii has honored his work. In 1985, Nakamine was invited by the American Gathering of Jewish Holocaust Survivors (Benjamin Meed, president) to attend a conference in Philadelphia. "During a conference dinner, I sat at a table with a sign saying, 'Dachau,' and people thought I was one of the survivors," smiled Nakamine.

The event that started it all decades ago is far more important than any single person, project or organization, he emphasized. "Preserving this history is not only for the veterans, but also for the Gold Star mothers, our children and future generations. The story belongs to history."

Exactly who was where at what time in or around Dachau may never be known. "It doesn't matter whether the 522nd soldiers were first, third, or sixteenth in arriving at Dachau," said Tanaka. "They were there."

DIFFERENT REVELATIONS and perspectives about World War II have appeared with each passing year, each passing decade. Consider the experience of Ruth Ishimoto, who met her husband Jerry in 1943, when she was interned in Arkansas and he was training with the 442nd. The Ishimotos were living in Okinawa during the 1970s when Ruth worked at the education office of the U.S. Marine Corps. "One day, I was talking to this Marine and I said, 'Oh, my husband was in World War II.' And he said, 'Which side was he on?'"

So it shouldn't have been a surprise when Bruce Yamashita, a bright young Japanese American lawyer, was drummed out of the United States Marine Corps Officer Candidate School (OCS) in 1989. Among the taunts he reportedly endured: "You speak English?" "We don't want your kind." "(During World War II) we whipped your Japanese ass."

There are, however, people who know and remember the men of the 100th/442nd. They come from such places as France, Germany, Texas and New York. The friendships among and between each other are warm, unbroken by time. They have exchanged letters, gifts, personal visits, wedding invitations, birth announcements and more. At gatherings in France, Texas, Hawaii, California and other places, the respect is there for all to see.

Yet, relatively few people know about the role of Japanese Americans during World War II and of their double bind of race and war. Raising the public's consciousness to a greater degree may start with the veterans themselves.

George Oiye, present at the rescue of the Lost Battalion and the liberation of prisoners at Dachau, summed up his feelings at a 1990 Japanese American veterans reunion in Kona, Hawaii: "I don't think any of us fully recognized the significance of the 100th/442nd's experiences at the time. Our children and grandchildren are going to hear things they haven't heard before, and I'm sure many questions will be raised. And that's good. Because they ought to know."

Index

Colonel Charles W. Pence, 442nd commander, is given a royal welcome at a July 1949 luau hosted by veterans of the combat team.

Lucy, found by 3rd Battalion medics in Luciana, Italy, was bedecked with a human dog tag and became a favorite mascot of the soldiers.

Bibliography

Books:

Anthony, J. Garner. *Hawaii Under Army Rule: The Real Story of Three Years of Martial Law in a Loyal American Territory.* Honolulu: University of Hawaii Press, 1976

Duus, Masayo Umezawa. *Unlikely Liberators.* Honolulu: University of Hawaii Press, 1987.

Fuchs, Lawrence. *Hawaii Pono: A Social History.* New York: Harcourt Brace Jovanovich, 1984.

Inouye, Daniel K., with L. Elliott. *Journey to Washington.* Englewood Cliffs, N.J.: Prentice-Hall, 1967.

Kotani, Roland. *The Japanese in Hawaii: A Century of Struggle.* Honolulu: Hawaii Hochi, Ltd., 1985.

Murayama, Milton. *All I Asking For Is My Body.* San Francisco: Supa Press, 1975.

Murphy, Thomas. *Ambassadors in Arms.* Honolulu: University of Hawaii Press, 1954.

Nakatsuka, Lawrence. *Hawaii's Own.* Honolulu: Hawaii's Own, 1946.

Odo, Franklin and Sinoto, Kazuko. *A Pictorial History of the Japanese in Hawaii, 1885-1924.* Honolulu: Hawaii Immigrant Heritage Preservation Center, Bishop Museum. Bishop Museum Press, 1985.

Prange, Gordon W. *At Dawn We Slept: The Untold Story of Pearl Harbor.* New York: Penguin Books, 1983.

Rademaker, John A. *These Are Americans.* Palo Alto, California: Pacific Books, 1951.

Shirey, Orville C. *Americans: The Story of the 442nd Combat Team.* Washington, D.C.: Infantry Journal Press, 1946.

Takaki, Ronald T. *Strangers From a Different Shore.* Boston: Little Brown, 1989.

Tanaka, Chester. *Go For Broke.* Richmond, California: Go For Broke, Inc., 1982.

Tsukano, John. *Bridge of Love.* Honolulu, Hawaii: Hawaii Hosts, Inc., 1985.

Booklets:

Americans of Japanese Ancestry and the United States Constitution. 1787-1987. San Francisco: National Japanese American Historical Society, 1987.

40th Anniversary 1942-1982: A Pictorial Report. Honolulu, Hawaii: Club 100, 1982

Dachau. County Town of Dachau. No date.

Go For Broke: The 442nd Decade, 10th Anniversary Reunion. Honolulu, Hawaii, July 20-31, 1953.

The Story of the 442nd Combat Team. Information-Education Section, MTOUSA, no date.

Supplement to United States Detention Camps Photo Exhibit 1990. San Francisco, California: National Japanese American Historical Society, 1990.

13th National Nisei Veterans Reunion—1982. Los Angeles, California, 1982.

Uncommon American Patriots. Seattle, Washington: Nisei Veterans Committee, March 1991.

Oba, Ronald. *The Men of Company F, 442nd Regimental Combat Team.* Honolulu, Hawaii, 1989.

Terry, John. *With Hawaii's AJA Boys at Camp Shelby, Mississippi.* Honolulu, Hawaii: Honolulu Star Bulletin, no date.

10th Anniversary Issue. The Hawaii Herald, Hawaii's Japanese American Journal. Honolulu, Hawaii: The Hawaii Herald, May 18, 1990.

Periodicals:

After the Battle. (London: Battle of Britain Prints International Ltd.) No. 27, 1980.

Go For Broke Bulletin. (Honolulu, Hawaii: 442nd Veterans Club) Issues:
vol. 36, no. 4, July-August 1984
vol. 41, no. 4, October-December 1990

The Hawaii Herald. Honolulu, Hawaii.

High Angle. Newspaper of the 522nd Field Artillery Battalion. World War II.

Yank. U.S. Army publication. World War II.

Honolulu Advertiser. Honolulu, Hawaii.

Honolulu Star-Bulletin. Honolulu, Hawaii.

NJAHS Focus. (San Francisco, California: National Japanese American Historical Society) Issues:
vol. 5, no. 4, July 1989
vol. 6, no. 2, March 1990
vol. 6, no. 3, May 1990
vol. 6, no. 6, November 1990

Puka-Puka Parade. (Honolulu, Hawaii: Club 100) Issues:
vol. 33, no. 2, April 1979
vol. 33, no. 3, September-October 1979
vol. 35, no. 2, March-April 1981
vol. 36, no. 3, July-August 1982
vol. 36, no. 6, November-December 1982
vol. 37, no. 3, July-September 1983

Films:

Ding, Loni. *Nisei Soldier*
Color of Honor

Schory, Kartiel. *Yankee Samurai*

Tsukano, John. Unreleased documentary on the 100th/442nd. Private screening.

Other Sources:

Akita, Stanley. Unpublished diary, "Stalag 7A," 1946.

Colliers Encyclopedia, 1989, vol. 7, p. 237.

Crost, Lyn. Letter to Secretary Ickes, June 17, 1945.

522nd Field Artillery Battalion Headquarters Journal, May 9, 1945

522nd declassified documents, Headquarters Battery, May 9, 1945

442nd Regimental Combat Team Headquarters Journal, October 29, 1944

Nakamine, Lorene. "A Journey Into the Past and Present," unpublished essay, 1977.

World Book Encyclopedia, 1991, vol. 21, pp. 485-486.

Yamada, Masao. Letter to Sherwood Dixon, October 30, 1944. Letter to Harrison Gerhardt, October 31, 1944.

Interviews:

Stan Akita, Alan Beekman, Tadao Beppu, Serge Carlesso, Josef Erbs, Yoshiaki Fujitani, Harold Fukunaga, Buck Glover, George Goto, George Hagiwara, Barney Hajiro, Joseph Hattori, Richard Hayashi, Takao Hedani, Royce Higa, Manabi Hirasaki, Lizo Honma, Eddie Ichiyama, Alvin Ihori, George Ikinaga, Daniel Inouye, Walter Inouye, George Ishihara, Jerry Ishimoto, Ruth Ishimoto, Susumu Ito, Kanemi Kanazawa, Stanley Kaneshiro, Shiro Kashino, Edward Kealanahele, Joe Kuroda, Taketo Kawabata, Tom Kawano, Young Oak Kim, Gilbert Kobatake, William Kochiyama, Arthur Komori, Hakobu Kumagai, Joe Kuroda, Richard Kurohara, Al Lipson, James Lovell, Walter Matsumoto, Shiro Matsuo, Harry McGowan, Yuki Minaga, George Mine, Oscar Miyashiro, Yuzuru Morita, Pierre Moulin, Neil Nagareda, Hideo Nakamine, Roy Nakamine, Donald Nakamura, Sally Nakamura, Wallace Nunotani, Joe Obayashi, George Oiye, Albert Oki, Kenzo Okubo, Yoshinao Omiya, Kenneth Otagaki, James Oura, William Ratcliffe, Henry Sakato, Matsuji Sakumoto, Robert Sasaki, Satoru Sawai, Kimie Shidaki, Joe Shimamura, Don Shimazu, Eiji Suyama, Minoru Suzumoto, Clarence Taba, Kiyoshi Takasaki, Michio Takata, Ben Tamashiro, Chester Tanaka, Robert Tanna, Edward Tarutani, John Tsukano, Ted Tsukiyama, Francis Tsuzuki, Harold Ueoka, Clifford Uyeda, Herbert Wong, Harold Yamada, Jim Yamashita, Harold Yokoyama, Kiyoshi Yoshimura, Israel Yost.

Photo & Art Credits

Endpapers: Rae Jacqueline Huo. **Pages 2, 3:** Courtesy, Susumu Ito. **Page 4:** Rae Jacqueline Huo. **Page 8:** Courtesy, National Japanese American Historical Society. **Page 10:** (Upper left) Photo by Herbert Sueoka, courtesy of 442nd Veterans Club. (Upper right) Courtesy, Lizo Honma. (Lower left) Courtesy, Joe Shimamura. (Lower right) Courtesy, Lizo Honma. **Page 12:** Courtesy, Walter Matsumoto. **Pages 14, 15:** Courtesy, Minoru Suzumoto. **Page 18:** Rae Jacqueline Huo. **Page 21:** (Upper left) Courtesy, George Oiye. (Upper right) Photo by Herbert Sueoka, courtesy of 442nd Veterans Club. (Lower left) Courtesy, Mrs. Masao Yamada. (Lower right) Courtesy, Joe Shimamura. **Pages 22, 23:** Rae Jacqueline Huo. **Page 26:** Courtesy, John Tsukano. **Pages 28, 29:** Illustration by Ralph Kagehiro. **Page 32:** Courtesy, George Goto. **Page 35:** Courtesy, Joe Kuroda and family. **Page 37:** Courtesy, Mrs. Masao Yamada. **Pages 42, 43:** Courtesy, Susumu Ito. **Page 47:** Courtesy, Barney Hajiro. **Pages 51, 53:** Courtesy, Mrs. Masao Yamada. **Page 54:** Courtesy, Susumu Ito. **Pages 56, 57:** Courtesy, John Tsukano. **Page 61:** From *Bridge of Love* by John Tsukano, Rendering by Steve Shrader. **Pages 62, 63:** Rae Jacqueline Huo. **Page 64:** Photo by Usaku Teragawachi, courtesy of Bishop Museum. **Page 69:** Courtesy, Hawaii State Archives. **Page 70:** Courtesy, Arakawas. **Page 74:** Courtesy, National Japanese American Historical Society. **Pages 78, 79:** Courtesy, U.S.S. Arizona Memorial, National Park Service. **Page 83:** Illustration by Ralph Kagehiro. **Page 86:** Black badge courtesy of Alvin Ihori, photo by Wayne Levin. **Page 89:** Courtesy, Visual Communications Archives, Los Angeles. **Pages 90, 91:** Photo by Toyo Miyatake, courtesy of National Japanese American Historical Society. **Page 95:** (Upper left) Courtesy, Shiro Kashino (Upper right) Courtesy, Ben Tamashiro. (Lower left) Courtesy, Taketo Kawabata. (Lower right) Courtesy, Roy Nakamine. **Page 99:** Courtesy, Ted Tsukiyama. **Page 100:** Courtesy, Dr. Franklin Kometani. **Page 103:** Courtesy, Bishop Museum. **Page 106:** Courtesy, Hawaii State Archives. **Pages 108, 109:** Rae Jacqueline Huo. **Page 111:** Courtesy, U.S. Signal Corps and Hideo Nakamine. **Page 112:** Courtesy, Lizo Honma. **Pages 114, 115:** Courtesy, Walter Inouye. **Page 117:** Courtesy, Lizo Honma. **Pages 122, 123:** Illustration by Ralph Kagehiro. **Page 125:** (Left) Courtesy, Mrs. Masao Yamada. (Right) Hideo Nakamine. **Page 127:** Courtesy, National Japanese American Historical Society. **Page 129:** Courtesy, Walter Inouye. **Page 132:** Courtesy, Mrs. Masao Yamada. **Page 134:** Courtesy, 1399th Veterans Club. **Page 135:** Courtesy, 1399th Veterans Club. **Pages 136, 137:** Map by Alexandru Preiss. **Page 140:** (Left) Courtesy, Kenneth Otagaki. (Right) Courtesy, Bessie Kawabata. **Page 141:** Photo by Herbert Sueoka, courtesy of 442nd Veterans Club. **Page 142:** Courtesy, Club 100 and Puka Puka Parade. **Page 143:** Courtesy, Colonel Young Oak Kim. **Page 147:** (Left) Courtesy, George Mine. (Right) Courtesy, Mrs. Masao Yamada. **Page 151:** (Left) Courtesy, Stanley Akita. (Right) Courtesy, Oscar Miyashiro. **Pages 156, 157:** Rae Jacqueline Huo. **Page 159:** Hideo Nakamine. **Pages 160, 161:** Courtesy, Lizo Honma. **Page 164:** Courtesy, Gilbert Nishimi. **Page 165:** Courtesy, Francis Tsuzuki. **Page 169:** Illustration by Ralph Kagehiro. **Pages 172, 173:** Courtesy, William Ratcliffe, C Battery, 522nd Field Artillery Battalion. **Page 175:** Courtesy, Joe Shimamura. **Page 177:** (Left) Courtesy, Walter Inouye. (Right) Courtesy, Royce Higa. **Page 181:** Courtesy, Joe Shimamura. **Pages 182, 183:** Courtesy, Gilbert Nishimi. **Page 184:** (Upper left) Courtesy, Mrs. Masao Yamada. (Upper right) Courtesy, Lizo Honma. (Lower left and right) Courtesy, Hideo Nakamine. **Page 185:** (Upper left and right) Lizo Honma. (Lower left) Photo by Herbert Sueoka, courtesy of 442nd Veterans Club. (Lower right) Courtesy, Hideo Nakamine. **Pages 186, 187:** Photo by Tajiro Uranaka. **Pages 191-197:** Courtesy, Robert Sasaki, Tadao Beppu, Hideo Nakamine. Lizo Honma, Royce Higa, Susumu Ito, Walter Inouye, Joe Shimamura. Color photos by Wayne Levin. **Page 200:** Courtesy, U.S. Army Museum of Hawaii. **Page 202:** Courtesy, National Japanese American Historical Society. **Page 203:** Courtesy, Mrs. Masao Yamada. **Page 206:** Courtesy, Walter Matsumoto. **Page 208:** Courtesy, U.S. Army Museum of Hawaii.

Reunited: Captain
Walter Matsumoto
with wife Hazel and
son Bruce, nearly five.
Honolulu, 1946.

Acknowledgements

NUMEROUS VETERANS, FRIENDS and even strangers graciously contributed their time and encouragement during the research and writing of this book. Only a few are listed here:

Special thanks to Hideo Nakamine and his wife, Kay. As chairman of the 522nd Dachau Research Committee of the 100th/442nd, Hideo guided me through smooth and rough times. I am also grateful to Robert Sasaki, executive secretary, 442nd Veterans Club, for hours of vital help at the clubhouse's "round table." Robert often looked at my worried face, saying, "Slow down, take it easy."

I appreciate the veterans, writers, friends, educators and others who gave of their hearts and minds to support this project. Robert Scott, my journalism mentor, endured long, late-night phone calls and provided valuable insights. Others baked pies, furnished legal counsel, fixed my computer, developed photos, trusted me with their albums and artifacts or donated their time. Alphabetically, they include: Goro Arakawa, Tadao Beppu, Wesley Ching, Tom Fairfull, Clarice Hashimoto, Richard Hayashi, Joseph and Florence Hattori, David Henna, Royce Higa, Manabi Hirasaki, Arnold Hiura, Lizo and Yvonne Honma, Walter and Martha Inouye, Susumu Ito, Mary Lou Jardine, Gilbert Kobatake, Shiro and Louise Kashino, Stanley Koki, Glenn Koons, Al Lipson, Daniel Martinez, Yuzuru Morita, Wallace Nunotani, Franklin Odo, Joe Obayashi, George Oiye, Keene Oka, Morio Omori, Kenneth Otagaki, Akira Sakima, Joe Shimamura, Minoru Suzumoto, Yoshito Takamine, Ben Tamashiro, Chester Tanaka, John Tasato, John Tsukano, Francis Tsuzuki, Clifford Uyeda, Daniel and Dorothy Valk, Jim Yamashita.

My gratitude to the staff of the: Clubs 100, 442nd, 1399th and MIS; U.S. Army Museum of Hawaii; Hawaii Herald; Spotlight Hawaii Publishing Co.; Waipahu Garden Cultural Park; Hawaii Okinawa Center; U.S.S. Arizona Memorial, National Park Service; Bishop Museum; State of Hawaii library system; State of Hawaii Archives; National Japanese American Historical Society (San Francisco); Japanese American National Museum (Los Angeles); Visual Communications (Los Angeles); Holocaust Research Center, Queensborough Community College (Brooklyn, New York).

Hardworking, creative people with high ethics and standards made this book possible: Steve Shrader, graphic artist; Cheryl Chee Tsutsumi, editor; Rae Huo and Wayne Levin, photographers; Ralph Kagehiro, illustrator; Alexandru Preiss, cartographer; Kathleen Cannallo, indexer-editorial assistant.

I can never thank enough my thoughtful husband, Lawrence, who understood it all.—T.C.

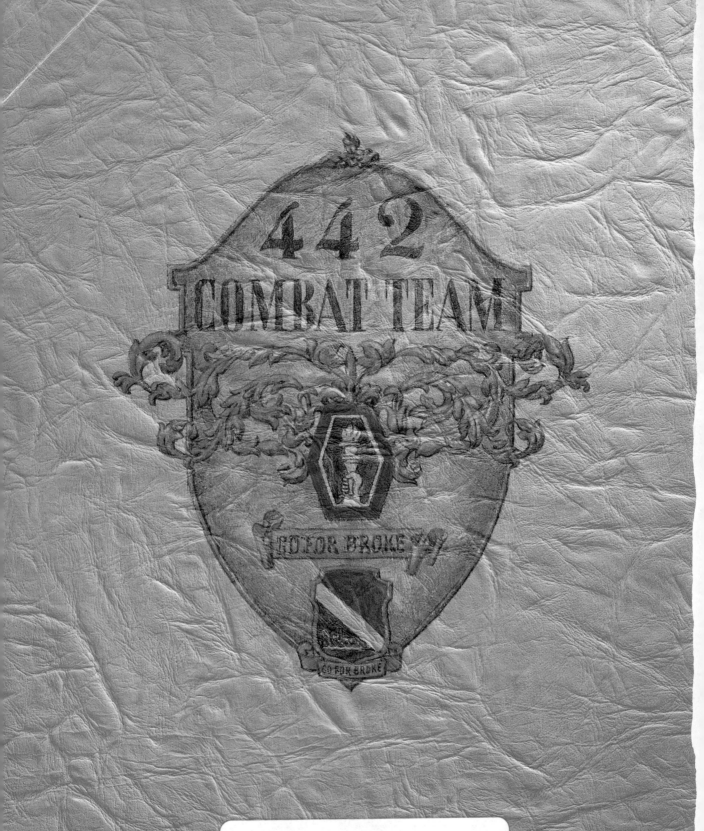